FOR THE DANDELION BLOWERS AND THE DAISY-
CHAIN WEAVERS, FOR THOSE WHO LOVE FLOWERS AND
ENJOY GOOD FOOD, THIS BOOK IS FOR YOU.

Many garden-variety flowers are not only lovely to look at, they're also unique additions to any meal. Curious to learn how? Just ask Nikki Fotheringham—gardener, home cook, and forager—who grows flowers in the meadow behind her house and turns them into edible products that she sells in her farm store. In *Taste Buds*, Nikki shares her recipes for baked goods like the Lemon Elderflower Cake, preserves like the Rose Jam (perfect on scones or alongside a charcuterie board), savory dishes like the Flower Pasta with Marigold Pesto, and wildflower drinks like the Lavender Love Martini. Inside, you'll find:

- **OVER 90 RECIPES FEATURING FLOWERS:** Each recipe highlights the natural flavors of flowers, all organized in stunning color-coded chapters.

- **A GUIDE TO 15 FLOWER VARIETIES:** Learn to identify and forage different flowers, from well-known favorites like hibiscus, lavender, peonies, and roses, to unexpected novelties like sumac, cornflowers, cattails, and more.

- **TIPS AND TRICKS FOR GROWING FLOWERS:** Make sure your garden sets you up for success in the kitchen with plenty of info on how to grow and care for your plants.

Whether you're an avid gardener, a foodie, or someone who simply adores flowers, you're sure to delight in *Taste Buds*.

Taste Buds

Taste Buds

A FIELD GUIDE TO COOKING AND BAKING WITH FLOWERS

NIKKI FOTHERINGHAM

appetite
by RANDOM HOUSE

Appetite by Random House™ and colophon are registered trademarks of Penguin Random House LLC.

Library and Archives of Canada Cataloguing in Publication is available upon request.

ISBN: 978-0-525-61219-3
eBook ISBN: 978-0-525-61220-9

Cover and book design by Emma Dolan
Cover and book photography by Laura Berman
Illustrations by Dana Harrison
Printed in China

Published in Canada by Appetite by Random House™, a division of Penguin Random House LLC.
www.penguinrandomhouse.ca

10 9 8 7 6 5 4 3 2 1

I dedicate this book to you, my dear reader. May you sip cocktails barefoot in the grass, chase fireflies in the summer meadow, find that hidden treasure and run away to a small cabin in the woods.

Contents

Introduction

I spent the first part of my life in Southern Africa, where a member of my family owned a plant nursery (they still do!). I spent my school vacations among the neat rows of plants with my cousin Sharon, who taught me everything I know and love about gardening. Bush crafting and foraging were a natural part of my daily life.

I took up cooking at age eight at the stove in the indoor kitchen and over the fire in the outdoor kitchen. When I was a teen, I lived in a tropical region. Little gray vervet monkeys visited our yard daily to raid the banana, guava and mango trees. It was from them that I learned that many of my favorite garden flowers were edible. My two great loves, gardening and cooking, were now one, and I have been cooking with flowers ever since.

These days, I live in a cedar wood in the heart of Ontario, Canada. It smells sweet in the spring, and sweeter still in the July heat. Three little creeks wind their way through the trees on my property, crossing over, joining, separating and generally babbling gleefully. On their banks grow elderberries and marsh marigolds.

At the edge of the wood is a meadow, which constantly changes its summer frocks thanks to the sky blue of the spring-flowering viper's bugloss, the summer's delicate white Queen Anne's lace and the stunning pink and purple fall asters.

I have always had a strong bond with nature. Flowers are a particular favorite of mine, but the deep, dark shade of a wood and the way flowing creek water slips over a fallen log are equally momentous for me. The natural world has been a constant source of joy, peace and wonder, and my greatest desire is to share this love with you. I want you to feel the deep calm of the old-growth trees, the restfulness of a slow-moving river and the love the animals and the plants have for you. Yes, you love nature, and it loves you right back.

I love the ephemeral nature of flowers—it forces you to slow down and smell them, because you know that tomorrow they'll be gone. One way for me to extend the wonder of flowers and to bring the natural world into your home is by sharing my favorite flower recipes with you.

This book is for the flower smellers, the dandelion blowers and the daisy-chain weavers. It's also for the pillow-fort architects, watermelon seed-spitting champions and breakfast chocolate cake aficionados. It is for everyone who loves the fleeting beauty of the rose because they understand there is nothing like the absence of flowers in the winter to make the heart grow fonder in the spring. To all who love to grow flowers, enjoy good food and feel the sunshine on their faces, this book is for you. . .

Foraging 101

Foraging was a part of everyday life not so long ago. I bet your grandma and great-grandma would forage for seasonal staples such as strawberries in the spring, and mushrooms and apples in the fall. It's a beautiful, rewarding art that I encourage you to revive in your own household.

The plants I've included in this book are common varieties that should be a piece of cake to identify. Most are found in gardens but some, like sumac and cattails, grow in the wild, and so you will need to forage for them.

Let's start with the first rule of foraging: don't eat any part of a plant unless you've made a positive identification of it. I've chosen fairly ubiquitous flowers that don't have poisonous doppelgangers, but always use the field guides at the beginning of each chapter to make a positive identification. If you're ever unsure, err on the side of caution and don't consume the plant.

Another rule of foraging is that it needs to be done with respect. When you forage properly, you don't leave the forests and meadows in a poorer state. Proper foraging can actually encourage growth in some plants. It should never lead to the disappearance of our favorite flowers.

The over-foraging of wild leeks (also known as ramps) is a classic example of what not to do. Ramps (*Allium tricoccum*) belong to the same family as onions and garlic but are not farmed. They are wild and ephemeral, with a very short season in the spring. When ramps became a popular gourmet ingredient, the wild ramp patches were overharvested by people who didn't know how to harvest responsibly. They were almost entirely eradicated throughout Canada. The areas where they grew were left exposed, often allowing invasive species to take hold.

Whatever plant you're harvesting, stick to these basic principles:

- **Forage only what you need and never damage the plant.**
- **Only harvest a maximum of 10 percent of the available bounty.**
- **Never harvest the first or last flowers you find (these are for the bees and other pollinators).**

Before you pick a flower, inspect it carefully and then shake it gently to ensure any bugs are set free. You can provide homes for bugs by leaving the leaves of the plants behind, as many bugs lay their eggs on the leaves. You can also install nests and bat boxes to increase habitat options for some of the locals.

You can also give back to the land by removing invasive species when you come across them and providing water, food and flowers for pollinators, birds and other woodland creatures.

Make sure you harvest your flowers in areas where they have not been exposed to pesticides, but if you're in any doubt, wash them thoroughly. Washing them in cold water will remove most pesticide residue, but you can make absolutely sure by adding 2 Tbsp (30 ml) baking soda and a squeeze of lemon juice to your rinsing water.

If you want to save the flowers for future use, you can gently pat them dry with a paper towel after washing and then freeze them in a freezer bag for up to three months.

You can also lay the clean flowers out on a paper towel to dry over several days. I press flowers between two sheets of paper towel and a couple of cookbooks to use as decorations on cakes and other baked goods.

The other thing to consider, especially in cities, is pets. Those park dandelions may look delectable, but they've probably been peed on by more than a couple of dogs, so I wouldn't recommend using them in a salad!

Responsibly living off the land has sustained our species for millions of years and, when done with respect, will keep the meadows and woodlands healthy and happy. You can enjoy a wonderfully beneficial and reciprocal relationship with your garden and all the creatures who call it home. I hope you will enjoy learning about edible flowers, harvesting them and bringing their beauty into your life.

When you're selecting plants for your garden, make sure they will thrive in your climate zone. Here's a quick guide to plant hardiness to help you choose.

HARDINESS ZONES

Zone	From	To	Zone	From	To
0a	< −65°F (−53.9°C)		7a	0°F (−17.8°C)	5°F (−15°C)
0b	−65°F (−53.9°C)	−60°F (−51.1°C)	7b	5°F (−15°C)	10°F (−12.2°C)
1a	−60°F (−51.1°C)	−55°F (−48.3°C)	8a	10°F (−12.2°C)	15°F (−9.4°C)
1b	−55°F (−48.3°C)	−50°F (−45.6°C)	8b	15°F (−9.4°C)	20°F (−6.7°C)
2a	−50°F (−45.6°C)	−45°F (−42.8°C)	9a	20°F (−6.7°C)	25°F (−3.9°C)
2b	−45°F (−42.8°C)	−40°F (−40°C)	9b	25°F (−3.9°C)	30°F (−1.1°C)
3a	−40°F (−40°C)	−35°F (−37.2°C)	10a	30°F (−1.1°C)	35°F (1.7°C)
3b	−35°F (−37.2°C)	−30°F (−34.4°C)	10b	35°F (1.7°C)	40°F (4.4°C)
4a	−30°F (−34.4°C)	−25°F (−31.7°C)	11a	40°F (4.4°C)	45°F (7.2°C)
4b	−25°F (−31.7°C)	−20°F (−28.9°C)	11b	45°F (7.2°C)	50°F (10°C)
5a	−20°F (−28.9°C)	−15°F (−26.1°C)	12a	50°F (10°C)	55°F (12.8°C)
5b	−15°F (−26.1°C)	−10°F (−23.3°C)	12b	55°F (12.8°C)	60°F (15.6°C)
6a	−10°F (−23.3°C)	−5°F (−20.6°C)	13a	60°F (15.6°C)	65°F (18.3°C)
6b	−5°F (−20.6°C)	0°F (−17.8°C)	13b	> 65°F (18.3°C)	

1. **GENUS:** *TARAXACUM OFFICINALE* **PERENNIAL**

IDENTIFICATION:

The dandelion has a surprisingly deep and thick white taproot that bleeds white when cut. The leaves are a deep, dark green and oblong, range from 3–10 inches (7–25 cm) long, and have jagged edges. The flowers grow on thin stems and are bright yellow with long, thin petals. The flowers, when pollinated, mature into fluffy white seed globes.

GROWING:

Dandelions prefer sunny, well-drained soil but will grow literally anywhere, from the cracks in pavements to the gutters you've been meaning to clean out one of these days. Dandelions are one of the most prolific and successful flowers around. While I'm sure you could buy dandelion seeds, you almost certainly don't need to. Simply clear a bit of the garden and leave it to its own devices.

After picking the flowers, shake out any bugs, then rinse and pat dry with a paper towel or leave out to dry.

Dandelions

The much-maligned dandelion should be revered as a god among flowers. Symbols of hope and happiness, these sunny little sweethearts should be given a little more love. Dandelion leaves, flowers and roots not only are edible (and delicious) but also provide a vital source of early pollen for bees.

The dandelion is known as the lover's oracle. This is because you can tell whether the object of your affection loves you or loves you not by blowing the seeds off a dandelion globe. If they are all gone in one breath, you are definitely loved. If many remain, it's a sad case of "loves you not." In addition, they are weather oracles. They shut their mature seed globes tightly when rain threatens.

While I have always loved the image of a dandy lion, the dandelion is actually named for the French "dent-de-lion," which is a literal translation of the Latin "dens leonis," or lion's tooth, thanks to the jagged edges of its leaves. Dandelion petals have a sweet, subtle, honey flavor that adds a fragrant flair to every dish.

. . . .

Be a weed eater! Dandelion greens are just amazing. They're best harvested in the spring when they're sweet and juicy, and they can be enjoyed in a salad or cooked like spinach. They are packed with vitamins A, C, E, and K and calcium.

. . . .

Dandelion Salad with Vinaigrette

Preheat the oven to 375°F (190°C).

To make the salad, wrap the beets in aluminum foil and bake until you can poke a fork in them without resistance, about 1 hour. Once the beets are cool enough to handle, peel them, cut them into 1-inch (2.5 cm) cubes and leave to cool completely.

Preheat the broiler to high.

Place the pumpkin seeds on a baking sheet and broil until golden brown and fragrant, about 10 minutes. Leave to cool.

Place the dandelion greens in a large serving bowl, then add the beets. Crumble the feta cheese overtop and garnish with the pumpkin seeds and dandelion petals.

To make the vinaigrette, place the ingredients in a small jug and mix to combine. Dress the salad just before serving.

TIPS: Use fresh greens that are pesticide free and have been washed thoroughly.

I roast beets when I am using the oven for something else. I can reheat them for hot meals, use a mandolin to slice them for pickles or make this delicious salad.

SERVES 6-8
Photo on page 47

FOR THE SALAD
3 medium beets
½ cup (125 ml) pumpkin seeds
8 cups (2 L) dandelion greens
   (washed and dried, see
   page 8)
½ cup (125 ml) crumbled
   feta cheese
½ cup (125 ml) dandelion
   petals (washed and dried,
   see page 8)

FOR THE VINAIGRETTE
½ cup (125 ml) extra virgin
   olive oil
3 Tbsp (45 ml) balsamic vinegar
1 Tbsp (15 ml) Dijon mustard
1 Tbsp (15 ml) maple syrup
2 cloves garlic, finely chopped
¼ tsp (1 ml) fine kosher salt
Freshly ground black pepper,
   to taste

This is a little time-consuming as the petals need to be removed from the green stems. In addition, the wine needs to mature for several months. But in the end you'll have golden, delicious dandelion wine, and if that's not worth a little waiting around, then what is?

. . . .

Dandelion Wine

Pour the boiling water into a large, heatproof bowl, add the dandelion petals and leave to steep for 5 minutes. Strain out the petals, but don't squeeze them or your wine will be bitter. Discard the petals. Leave the water to cool to 90°F (30°C) so the yeast will work.

Stir the yeast into the cooled water, followed by the sugar, orange slices and lemon slices. Pour the mixture into a 32–40 cup (8–10 L) container with a fermentation lock. The lock will allow gas caused by the fermentation process to escape without letting bacteria or dust in.

Let the wine ferment in a cool place until the bubbles stop. This should take 10–14 days, depending on the temperature of the room you store it in. Once the mixture has stopped bubbling, gently pour out the wine into a sealable container, leaving the bottom sediment and fruit behind. Pour slowly and carefully. There will inevitably be a little sediment that finds its way in, but try to keep as much of it out as you can.

Leave the wine to ferment for another 30 days in a cool, dry place, lifting the lid from time to time to burp it in case there is residual gas. Next, gently pour the wine through a cheesecloth into a clean large container to filter it. Take care to leave the yeast sediment behind.

Bottle your wine in sterilized bottles and leave to age another 6–9 months before enjoying.

MAKES SIX 3-CUP (750 ML) BOTTLES

Photo on page 103

4 quarts (4 L) boiling water

4 cups (1 L) dandelion petals, washed and dried (see page 8)

1 envelope (5g) wine yeast (find this online or at wine supply stores)

8 cups (2 L) granulated sugar

1 orange, sliced

1 lemon, sliced

Pound cakes date all the way back to the early 18th century and contain the building blocks of all great cakes: butter, flour, sugar and eggs. Traditionally, a pound cake would consist of one pound of each of the four main ingredients, hence the name. You can make it in a 9 × 5-inch (23 × 13-inch) loaf pan for a more traditional pound cake if you prefer. I use a Bundt pan because I just love to say "Bundt cake" and tend to opt for Bundt pans whenever bundting possible.

. . . .

Dandelion Pound Cake

Preheat the oven to 325°F (160°C). Grease and flour a Bundt pan.

To make the cake, sift the flour, baking powder and salt into a bowl and gently mix in the dandelion petals.

Using a stand mixer fitted with the paddle attachment, cream the butter with the sugar on medium speed until light and fluffy, about 3 minutes. Add the eggs one at a time, beating well after each addition. Add the vanilla and mix well to combine, about 2 minutes.

Alternate adding the flour mixture and the milk to the butter mixture, beginning and ending with the flour mixture. Mix for about 2 minutes, scraping down the sides and bottom of the bowl as needed. Once the batter is combined, pour it into the prepared Bundt pan.

Bake until a skewer inserted into the cake center comes out clean, 45–55 minutes. Place the pan on a wire rack. Leave the cake to cool in the pan for 10 minutes, then carefully turn it out onto a cake plate.

To make the icing, place the ingredients in a medium bowl and whisk until smooth. Pour over the cake to cover it evenly. Alternatively, you can sprinkle the cake with 2 Tbsp (30 ml) icing sugar.

Store any leftover cake in an airtight container in the fridge for 3–4 days.

MAKES ONE 10-INCH (25 CM) BUNDT CAKE

Photo on page 15

FOR THE CAKE

2½ cups (625 ml) all-purpose flour

1½ tsp (7 ml) baking powder

Pinch fine kosher salt

¼ cup (60 ml) dandelion petals, washed and dried (see page 8)

1¼ cups (300 ml) unsalted butter, at room temperature

1¾ cups (425 ml) granulated sugar

4 large eggs

1½ tsp (7 ml) pure vanilla extract

⅔ cup (150 ml) whole milk

FOR THE ICING (OPTIONAL)

1 cup (250 ml) icing sugar

Zest of 1 lemon

1 Tbsp (15 ml) lemon juice

1 Tbsp (15 ml) whole milk

Is there anything more whimsically jolly than an upside-down cake? Turning it over to reveal the fruity underside really turns up the wow factor. I love eating this cake barefoot and in the company of loved ones for no particular reason.

. . . .

Dandelion Upside-Down Pear Cake

Preheat the oven to 350°F (175°C). Grease a 9-inch (23 cm) round cake pan and line it with parchment paper.

To make the pear layer, mix together the sugar, butter and lemon juice in a small pot and set over medium heat. Heat, stirring constantly, just until the sugar is dissolved, about 2 minutes. Pour the liquid sugar into the prepared pan, tipping the pan so that the bottom is evenly covered. Sprinkle the dandelion petals overtop.

Peel and core the pears, and then thinly slice them lengthwise. Arrange them, slightly overlapping, on top of the sugar mixture and dandelion petals.

To make the cake, sift the flour, baking powder, baking soda and salt into a bowl and gently mix in the dandelion petals.

Using a stand mixer fitted with the paddle attachment, cream the butter with both the sugars on medium-high speed until light and fluffy, about 5 minutes. Add the eggs one at a time, beating well after each addition. Add the vanilla and mix well to combine, about 2 minutes. Scrape down the bottom and sides of the bowl as needed.

Alternate adding the flour mixture and the buttermilk to the butter mixture, beginning and ending with the flour mixture. Mix for about 2 minutes, scraping down the sides and bottom of the bowl as needed. Once the batter is combined, pour it over your pears.

continues

MAKES ONE 9-INCH (23 CM) CAKE

Photo on page 15

FOR THE PEARS

½ cup (125 ml) packed
   brown sugar
¼ cup (60 ml) unsalted butter
2 tsp (10 ml) freshly squeezed
   lemon juice
¼ cup (60 ml) fresh dandelion
   petals, washed and dried
   (see page 8)
3 firm ripe pears (any type)

FOR THE CAKE

1⅓ cups (325 ml) all-purpose
   flour
1½ tsp (7 ml) baking powder
½ tsp (2 ml) baking soda
Pinch coarse kosher salt
¼ cup (60 ml) dandelion petals
   (washed and dried, see page 8)
½ cup (125 ml) unsalted butter
⅓ cup (75 ml) granulated sugar
⅓ cup (75 ml) packed brown
   sugar
2 large eggs
1 tsp (5 ml) pure vanilla extract
¾ cup (175 ml) buttermilk

Bake until a skewer inserted into the cake layer comes out clean, about 40 minutes. Place the pan on a wire rack. Leave the cake to cool completely in the pan.

Save the big reveal until you are ready to serve. Place a plate over the pan, flip it over, remove the pan and parchment paper, and ta-da! Beautiful caramelized pear cake!

Store any leftover cake in an airtight container in the fridge for 3–4 days.

TIP: Break the petals off fresh dandelions for this recipe in the summer, but be sure that they have not been exposed to pesticides and wash to remove dirt and bugs before using. I dry whole flowers in the summer for use in the winter months. You can also freeze dandelion flowers in the summer for winter use.

DANDELION POUND CAKE
(page 12)

DANDELION UPSIDE-DOWN
PEAR CAKE (page 13)

DANDELION JAMMY DODGERS
(page 17)

Dandelions make excellent jams thanks to their gentle, sweet taste. I love these little jars of sunshine. In fact, the dandelion is said to represent all celestial bodies. The flower for the sun, the globe of seeds for the moon and the individual seeds are the stars as they are scattered across the skies.

Dandelion Jam

Put the boiling water in a large heatproof bowl, add the dandelion flowers and leave to steep for at least 2 hours (overnight is better) to make dandelion tea. Strain out the flowers, but don't squeeze them or your jam will be bitter. Pull off some of the petals of about 4 flowers and add them to the dandelion tea. Discard the remaining petals.

Prepare your jars for canning by boiling them in a canning pot for 10 minutes. Using long tongs or a jar lifter, transfer the jars to a wire rack and allow to cool.

Place the dandelion tea in a large pot and mix in the lemon juice and pectin. Bring to a rolling boil over high heat and add the sugar all at once and stir to dissolve. Bring to a boil again, still on high heat, and stir for 1 minute. Remove the pot from the stove and continue to stir until the sugar has melted completely, about 5 minutes. Scoop the froth off the top of the jam and discard.

Spoon the jam into the jars and seal the lids firmly. Check the water level in your canning pot, place the jars back in the pot and boil them for 10 minutes. Using long tongs or a jar lifter, transfer the jars to a wire rack to cool.

This jam keeps on the shelf for 1 year and for 1 month in the fridge after opening.

MAKES 5–6 CUPS
(1.25–1.5 L)
Photo on page 48

4 cups (1 L) boiling water
2 cups (500 ml) fresh dandelion
   flowers, washed and dried
   (see page 8)
1 tsp (5 ml) freshly squeezed
   lemon juice
1 (1¾ oz/49 g) package
   powdered pectin
4 cups (1 L) granulated sugar,
   or more to taste

TIP: Dry out dandelion flowers in the summer to use in jam through the winter. Frozen flowers also work well for this.

Jammy dodgers are a traditional British shortbread sandwich cookie with a jam filling. The top cookie has a little cutout through which the jam oozes invitingly. They are sure to become as firm a favorite in your home as they are in mine.

. . . .

Dandelion Jammy Dodgers

Sift the flour, sugar and salt into in a large bowl. Using your fingertips, rub in the butter until the mixture resembles breadcrumbs. In a separate bowl, beat the egg yolks and vanilla together and then add to the flour mixture. Mix until the dough comes together, being careful not to overwork it. On a lightly floured surface, roll out the dough to ¼ inch (½ cm) thick.

Use a 2½-inch (6.5 cm) cookie cutter to cut out 40 cookies and use a smaller 1 ¾-inch (4.5cm) cookie cutter to punch out the centers of half of the cookies. Place all the pieces on a greased baking sheet and put them in the fridge to firm up, about 10 minutes.

Preheat the oven to 350°F (175°C).

Bake until the edges just start to brown but the cookies are otherwise still pale, 10–12 minutes. Place the baking sheet on a wire rack and let the cookies cool completely.

Once the cookies have cooled, use about 1 tsp (5 ml) jam per cookie to sandwich the two halves together.

Store the cookies in an airtight container at room temperature for up to 3 days

MAKES 20 SANDWICH COOKIES
Photo on page 15

2 cups (500 ml) all-purpose flour
1 cup (250 ml) icing sugar
Pinch coarse kosher salt
1 cup + 2 Tbsp (280 ml) cold salted butter, cut in cubes
2 large egg yolks
2 tsp (10 ml) pure vanilla extract
½ cup (125 ml) Dandelion Jam (page 16)

TIP: The dough should be soft, but if it's too sticky, add 1 Tbsp (15 ml) of flour before you roll it out.

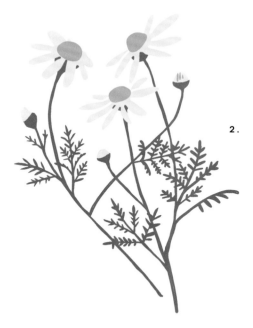

2.

2. GENUS: *MATRICARIA RECUTITA*   **PERENNIAL**

. . . .

IDENTIFICATION:

Chamomile is a low-growing plant with bipinnate feathery leaves and composite flowers. Bipinnate means each leaf divides into smaller leaf sections, and a composite flower is one that is made up of many simpler flowers. Chamomile comes in two main varieties: German and Roman. They both produce pretty daisy-like flowers with white petals and a yellow center. German chamomile is most often used to make tea while Roman has a sweeter smelling bloom.

Both types will grow to 8–24 inches (20–60 cm) tall and wide.

GROWING:

Chamomile is happy wherever it finds itself, but it prefers full sun and well-drained soil. Sow seeds directly into the soil after the last frost. Water them well with at least 1 inch (2.5 cm) of water a week until the plants are established. They should begin to flower 10 weeks after planting. Once chamomile is established it's quite drought-tolerant, but water it during extremely hot or dry periods.

Harvest the flowers when they are fully opened and dry them out to use in recipes and teas. I like to shake out any bugs, gently wash the flowers and pat them dry with a dish towel. Lay them out on a paper towel in a warm, sunny place to dry. You can use the fresh petals for decoration. If you leave half the flowers in place at the end of summer, the plants should self-seed.

Chamomile

The word "chamomile" comes from the Greek "chamaimēlon" meaning "ground apple." Chamomile symbolizes peace and calm, renewal and rebirth. It's known for its ability to bloom for long periods during the summer months and its resistance to damage from foot traffic.

Chamomile has been used through the ages as a medicinal herb and as a bittering agent by beer-making monks. Its scent fends off bugs, and the monks noticed that when it is planted next to ailing plants, it restores and heals them. Steep a couple of chamomile teabags in hot water over-night, pop your strong tea into a spray bottle and you have a natural pest repellant for the garden.

The chamomile patch on my farm is gargantuan. Every morning in the summer, before the sun reaches it, I crawl among the beautifully scented flowers and harvest those that are fully opened. The smell and beauty of these sweet little blooms ensure a very good start to the day!

. . . .

CHAMOMILE CARROT SOUP 20

DUTCH BABY 21

CHAMOMILE CUSTARD PIE 23

CHAMOMILE LATTE 25

CHAMOMILE HOT TODDY 25

LEMON POPPY SEED BUNDT CAKE 28

SALTED HONEY CHAMOMILE CAKE 29

CHAMOMILE MACARONS 32

This is a quick, easy soup recipe that makes a great lunch or an excellent appetizer. Serve it with chunks of warm, buttered bread on rainy days for best results.

. . . .

Chamomile Carrot Soup

Put the boiling water in a large heatproof bowl, add the chamomile flowers and leave to steep for 10 minutes.

Meanwhile, place the oil in a large pot and warm it over low heat. Add the onions, ginger and garlic and fry, stirring frequently, until the onions become translucent, about 10 minutes.

While the onions are frying, strain out the chamomile flowers from the water, but don't squeeze them or the water will be bitter. Discard the flowers. Set the chamomile water aside.

Add the turmeric and paprika to the onions and fry until the spices begin to stick, about 2 minutes. Pour in the chamomile water and then add the carrots, zest, salt and honey. Using a wooden spoon, deglaze the pan.

Turn up the heat to medium and bring the mixture to a boil. Turn down the heat to low and simmer, uncovered, stirring occasionally until the carrots are soft, about 10 minutes. Turn off the heat completely.

Using an immersion blender, blend the soup in the pot until smooth. Taste and balance your flavors with the lemon juice and more salt if needed.

SERVES 4

Photo on page 116

5 cups (1.25 L) boiling water
20 dried chamomile flowers
   (see page 18), or 2 chamomile
   tea bags
¼ cup (60 ml) extra virgin
   olive oil
2 red onions, chopped
2-inch (5 cm) piece of ginger,
   peeled and finely chopped
2 cloves garlic, crushed
1 tsp (5 ml) ground turmeric
1 tsp (5 ml) paprika
3 cups (750 ml) chopped
   carrots
Zest of ½ lemon
⅛ tsp (0.5 ml) coarse kosher salt
1 tsp (5 ml) honey
Freshly squeezed lemon juice,
   to taste

TIP: For a vegan option, sweeten the soup with maple syrup instead of honey.

I've never met a pancake I didn't like. You've got your classic stack, drizzled in syrup. Then there's the French crepe, flapjacks and crumpets. And of course, the Dutch baby—a sort of puffed-up pancake bowl you can fill with fruit. This baby is the lovechild of a crepe and a pancake and turns any breakfast into an instant party.

. . . .

Dutch Baby

Place the milk in a small pot and gently warm it over medium heat. Add the chamomile. Remove the pot from the heat just before the milk reaches a boil and leave to steep for 10 minutes. Strain out the chamomile, but don't squeeze it or the milk will be bitter. Discard the chamomile. Pour the milk into a large mixing bowl. Set aside to cool completely.

Add the eggs, flour, sugar, vanilla and salt to the chamomile milk and mix until a smooth batter forms. Let the batter rest, uncovered, at room temperature for 15 minutes.

Preheat the oven to 400°F (200°C). Place a large cast-iron skillet in the oven to heat while the oven comes to temperature.

Once the skillet is hot, remove it carefully and place the butter in it to melt. Swirl the skillet to coat the bottom and sides of the pan, then pour in the batter and return the skillet to the oven. Bake until the Dutch baby has puffed up and is browning around the edges, 15–20 minutes.

As you remove the Dutch baby from the oven, the air will escape and the batter will sink down to form a bowl shape. Dust with icing sugar and drizzle with maple syrup. Cut into wedges and serve hot, or fill with fruit and whipped cream and then cut into wedges to serve.

SERVES 4

Photo on page 56

¾ cup (175 ml) whole milk

20 dried chamomile flowers (see page 18), or 2 chamomile tea bags

3 large eggs

½ cup (125 ml) all-purpose flour

2 Tbsp (30 ml) granulated sugar

½ tsp (2 ml) pure vanilla extract

½ tsp (2 ml) coarse kosher salt

3 Tbsp (45 ml) unsalted butter

Icing sugar, for dusting

Maple syrup, for drizzling

Fresh fruit and whipped cream

CHAMOMILE CUSTARD
PIE (page 23)

CHAMOMILE LATTE
(page 25)

Don't you love it when a flan comes together? To say that custard pie, aka milk tart, is my favorite dessert is the understatement of the century. I just know that you're going to love it, because it's super easy to make and it will level up your teatime pie game.

. . . .

Chamomile Custard Pie

To make the crust, combine the flour and salt in a large bowl. Using your fingertips, rub in the shortening until the mixture resembles bread crumbs. Add the vinegar and just enough cold water to bring the dough together, being careful not to overwork it. Turn out the dough, shape it into a disk, cover it with plastic wrap and refrigerate for at least 30 minutes.

Preheat the oven to 400°F (200°C). Grease a 9-inch (23 cm) pie dish and line it with parchment paper.

On a lightly floured surface, roll out the dough to a 12-inch (30 cm) circle, then carefully transfer it to the pie dish. Gently work it into the edges and up the sides of the dish, and trim off the excess. Prick the bottom of the dough 7–10 times with a fork, then line loosely with parchment paper and fill to the brim with baking beans or pie weights. Blind bake the pie shell until the edges start to brown, 7–10 minutes. Set aside to cool.

To make the filling, place the milk and chamomile in a medium pot and warm the milk over medium heat until hot but not boiling.

Meanwhile, place the sugar, flour, cornstarch, salt, eggs, butter and vanilla in a medium mixing bowl and whisk until smooth.

continues

MAKES ONE 9-INCH (23 CM) PIE
Photo on page 22

FOR THE CRUST

1⅓ cups (325 ml) all-purpose flour

½ tsp (2 ml) coarse kosher salt

½ cup (125 ml) vegetable shortening

½ tsp (2 ml) white vinegar

Cold water

When the milk is hot, strain out the chamomile, but don't squeeze the flowers or the milk will be bitter, and return the pot to the heat. Discard the chamomile.

Add about one-quarter of the hot milk to the butter mixture and mix to temper it, then slowly pour the warmed butter mixture into the pot of hot milk, whisking as you go so no lumps form. Heat, stirring constantly, until the mixture thickens (this should only take a few seconds). Remove the pot from the heat and pour the mixture into the pie shell. Sprinkle the cinnamon overtop of the custard. Place the pie, uncovered, in the fridge until set.

Store any leftover pie in an airtight container in the fridge for 1–2 days.

FOR THE CUSTARD FILLING

4 cups (1 L) whole milk

20 dried, crushed chamomile
   flowers (see page 18), or
   2 chamomile tea bags

½ cup (125 ml) granulated sugar

3 Tbsp (45 ml) all-purpose flour

3 Tbsp (45 ml) cornstarch

Pinch coarse kosher salt

2 large eggs

2 Tbsp (30 ml) butter

1 tsp (5 ml) pure vanilla extract

1 Tbsp (15 ml) ground cinnamon

The narcoleptic combination of warm milk and chamomile makes for a dreamy hug in a teacup. Don't operate heavy machinery after one of these. Instead, curl up in a cozy spot and drift away to Dreamland.

· ·

Chamomile Latte

Place the chamomile flowers and cardamom pods in a small pot and add the milk. Gently warm the milk over medium heat until hot but not boiling (or use a milk frother for a frothy latte). Remove from the heat and pour the milk through a small sieve into a mug. Discard the chamomile flowers and cardamom pods.

Sweeten with honey and sprinkle cinnamon on top.

TIP: Feel free to use plant-based milks and substitute maple syrup for the honey for a vegan option.

SERVES 1

Photo on page 22

20 dried chamomile flowers
   (see page 18), or 2 chamomile
   tea bags
6 cardamom pods
1 cup (250 ml) whole milk
Honey, to taste
Ground cinnamon, for sprinkling

Around the tail end of January, when the thrill of snow and sweaters has long since worn off, I get the winter blues. Luckily, I have a secret weapon that warms the cockles of my heart and gets me feeling all comfy-cozy. This hot toddy is best consumed when you're in your PJs and ready for bed.

· ·

Chamomile Hot Toddy

Place the water in a small pot and bring to a boil over high heat. Turn off the heat and add the chamomile, cinnamon stick and cloves. Steep for 5 minutes. Pour the liquid through a small sieve into a mug. Discard the herbs and add the whiskey plus honey and lemon juice to taste. Garnish with a slice of lemon and enjoy!

SERVES 1

Photo on page 27

¾ cup (175 ml) water
10 dried chamomile flowers (see
   page 18), or 1 chamomile tea bag
1 cinnamon stick
3 cloves
1½ oz (45 ml) whiskey
Honey, to taste
Freshly squeezed lemon juice,
   to taste
Slice of lemon

LEMON POPPY SEED
BUNDT CAKE
(page 28)

CHAMOMILE HOT TODDY
(page 25)

This cake makes me happy. It's not overly sweet and the zing of the lemon married with the nutty poppy seed flavor produces a deliciously complex teatime treat. Did you know that a single gram of poppy seeds contains a whopping 3,300 seeds?

. . . .

Lemon Poppy Seed Bundt Cake

Preheat the oven to 350°F (180°C). Spray a Bundt pan with cooking spray.

Sift the flour, baking powder and baking soda into a large bowl and gently mix in the chamomile flowers and poppy seeds.

Using a stand mixer fitted with the paddle attachment, cream the butter with the sugar on high speed until light and fluffy, about 5 minutes. Add the eggs one at a time, beating well after each addition. Scrape down the sides and bottom of the bowl as needed. Add the lemon juice and zest, oil and vanilla. Mix well to combine, about 3 minutes.

Alternate slowly adding the flour mixture and the sour cream to the butter mixture, beginning and ending with the flour mixture. Mix for about 2 minutes, scraping down the sides and bottom of the bowl as needed again. When the batter is combined, pour it into the prepared Bundt pan.

Bake until a skewer inserted into the cake comes out clean, about 50 minutes. Leave to cool in the pan for 15 minutes then place your cake plate over the Bundt pan and gently turn it over. Remove the pan and leave the cake to cool completely.

Store any leftover cake in an airtight container in the fridge for 3–4 days.

MAKES ONE BUNDT CAKE TO SERVE 12 (OR 1, NO JUDGMENT)

Photo on page 26

2¾ cups (675 ml) all-purpose
 flour
1 tsp (5 ml) baking powder
½ tsp (2 ml) baking soda
20 dried chamomile flowers,
 crushed (see page 18), or
 2 chamomile tea bags
⅓ cup (75 ml) poppy seeds
¾ cup (175 ml) salted butter,
 at room temperature
2 cups (500 ml) granulated sugar
4 large eggs, at room temperature
⅓ cup (75 ml) freshly squeezed
 lemon juice (about 2 lemons)
Zest of 1 lemon
¼ cup (60 ml) vegetable oil
2 tsp pure vanilla extract
1 cup (250 ml) Full-fat sour cream

TIP: Make a glaze with 1 cup (250 ml) icing sugar, 1 Tbsp (15 ml) lemon juice, the zest of 1 lemon and 1 Tbsp (15 ml) milk in a small bowl. Whisk until smooth and pour over the cake.

This is a special occasion cake. I make it most often for big-ticket events like birthdays, graduations and weddings. But you can also make it to celebrate smaller events, like the first crocus flower in spring, getting all the laundry done or just generally crushing it. It is also an excellent breakfast cake. If you ask me, the very best thing about it is the salted honey. Salt enhances the flavors of other foods, especially sweet ones. The usually subtle delicacy of honey gets such a boost from the sea salt that you'll be eating the frosting with a spoon (which is perfectly acceptable, of course).

Salted Honey Chamomile Cake

To make the cake, place the milk in a small pot and bring it to a simmer over medium heat. Do not let it come to a boil. Turn off the heat and add the chamomile. Leave to steep until the milk is room temperature. Strain out the chamomile, but do not squeeze it or the milk might taste bitter. Discard the chamomile. Set the milk aside.

Preheat the oven to 350°F (175°C). Grease two 9-inch (23 cm) round cake pans.

Sift the flour, salt, baking powder and baking soda into a large bowl.

Using a stand mixer fitted with the paddle attachment, cream the butter with the sugar on high speed until light and fluffy, about 5 minutes. Add the eggs, egg whites and vanilla and mix well to combine, about 2 minutes. Scrape down the bottom and sides of the bowl as needed.

Alternate adding the flour mixture and the milk to the butter mixture, beginning and ending with the flour mixture. You want everything to be just mixed in for this batter. Scrape down the sides and bottom of the bowl as needed. Once the batter is combined, pour it into the prepared cake pans.

continues

MAKES ONE DOUBLE-LAYER 9-INCH (23 CM) CAKE
Photo on page 31

FOR THE CAKE

1½ cups (375 ml) whole milk

40 crushed, dried chamomile flowers (see page 18), or 4 chamomile tea bags

3⅔ cups (900 ml) all-purpose flour

1 tsp (5 ml) fine kosher salt

2 tsp (10 ml) baking powder

¾ tsp (4 ml) baking soda

1½ cups (375 ml) unsalted butter, at room temperature

2 cups (500 ml) granulated sugar

3 large eggs + 2 large egg whites, at room temperature

1 Tbsp (15 ml) pure vanilla extract

Bake until a skewer inserted into the center of each cake comes out clean, 25–30 minutes. Place the cake pans on wire racks and let the cakes cool completely in the pans.

To make the frosting, using a stand mixer fitted with a paddle attachment, cream the butter with the icing sugar, salt, honey and lemon juice on medium speed until light and fluffy, about 5 minutes.

Once the cakes are cool, remove them from the pans. Place one cake layer on a cake stand and top it with about one-third of the buttercream. Sandwich the second layer on top. Now use the remaining frosting to cover the outside of your cake.

You can decorate it as you wish, but if you have fresh, edible flowers, they add a splash of color and pizzazz. You can use chamomile flowers or whatever you have on hand.

Store the cake in an airtight container in the fridge for up to 3 days.

FOR THE FROSTING

¼ cup (60 ml) salted butter, at room temperature

1 cup (250 ml) icing sugar

¼ tsp (1 ml) sea salt

2 Tbsp (30 ml) honey

1 Tbsp (15 ml) freshly squeezed lemon juice

SALTED HONEY
CHAMOMILE CAKE

Macarons are the ultimate indulgence. With the perfect macaron, the meringue should melt the minute it hits your mouth, leaving only the sweet center to linger on your tongue. It should be like eating a rainbow while sitting on a unicorn and having your toes licked by kittens. (Note that you need to get your egg whites ready 2 hours before you plan to bake these.)

Chamomile Macarons

Before you begin, wash the bowl and whisk attachment of your stand mixer in warm soapy water and rinse thoroughly. If there is any grease on your equipment, your egg whites won't whip up properly.

To make the macarons, line a baking sheet with parchment paper. If you want uniform macarons, use a small cookie cutter or shot glass to draw 1¼–1½-inch (3–3.5-cm) circles on the parchment paper to use as a guide when piping. Fit your piping bag with a large, round tip.

Using a food processor fitted with the steel blade, blitz the icing sugar, almond flour and chamomile for 2 minutes to ensure the dry ingredients are as fine as possible. Sift the mixture into a large bowl.

Using a stand mixer fitted with the whisk attachment, whip the egg whites, vanilla, cream of tartar and salt on medium speed until soft peaks form. Add the superfine sugar 1 Tbsp (15 ml) at a time, mixing well between additions. When all of the sugar is in, turn up the speed to medium-high and whip until stiff peaks form, about 5 minutes.

Using a spatula, fold in the almond mixture, about 2 Tbsp (30 ml) at a time bit at a time, until completely incorporated.

MAKES 30 MACARONS

Photo on page 71

FOR THE MACARONS

1¾ cups (425 ml) icing sugar

1 cup (250 ml) almond flour

10 dried chamomile flowers (see page 18), or 1 chamomile tea bag

3 large egg whites, left, covered, at room temperature for 2 hours before using

½ tsp (2 ml) pure vanilla extract

¼ tsp (1 ml) cream of tartar

⅛ tsp (0.5 ml) table salt

¼ cup (60 ml) superfine sugar

FOR THE FILLING

½ cup (125 ml) salted butter

¼ cup (60 ml) dried chamomile flowers, or 4 chamomile tea bags

2 cups (500 ml) icing sugar, sifted

Fill the piping bag with the batter (see tip, page 42) and pipe circles onto the parchment paper. Dip your finger in water and gently press down on any peaks that form on top of the macarons during piping.

Leave the macarons to dry at room temperature until a thin film forms overtop, up to 2 hours.

About 20 minutes before the end of the drying time, preheat the oven to 300°F (150°C).

Bake the macarons for 14 minutes or until they form little bubbly feet. You can test for doneness by carefully touching a top (it's hot!) and if it's firm, they're ready. Place the baking sheet on a wire rack and let the macarons cool completely.

To make the filling, place the butter in a small pot and melt over low heat. Remove from heat and gently mix in the chamomile and steep for 10 minutes. Strain out the chamomile, but don't squeeze it or the mixture will be bitter. Discard the chamomile.

Place the butter in the fridge until it just starts to solidify. You want it to be soft, but not watery. Place the butter and icing sugar in a small bowl and whisk until smooth. Sandwich 2 macarons together with the chamomile filling. Pop one in your mouth immediately.

Store the macarons in an airtight container in the fridge for up to 1 week.

TIP: Add a gel food coloring to your batter when folding in the dry ingredients for colored macrons.

3.

3. GENUS: *SAMBUCUS*   PERENNIAL

. . . .

IDENTIFICATION:

Elderflowers are a creamy white color and grow in great big umbrella sprays. Each bunch is made up of many tiny flowers with five petals and a ton of yellow pollen on the stamens, which stick out on little stalks.

The leaves have a serrated edge and appear in groups of five on the stem. Elder trees don't have a central trunk. Instead, they have scraggly stems that grow out to reach the sunshine.

GROWING:

Elder trees love moist, well-drained soil and full to part sun. They enjoy a good fertilizer in early spring before the leaves come out. They benefit from a hard prune in the fall in their first three years. This encourages more stems to grow for a fuller, healthier tree. Elder trees need 1 inch (2.5 cm) of water every week in order to bloom and fruit. You can irrigate or water them if there isn't enough rainfall to do the job.

To harvest the flowers, gently shake the bunches to release any bugs back into the wild, then rinse them and leave them to dry on a paper towel in a warm, dry spot. Using a fork, comb through the bunches to separate the flowers from their stems. Discard the stems and then use the flowers or dry them for use in the winter. Store in an airtight container.

Elderflower

Elderflowers bloom in late May and early June. They are small and sweet, have a gentle fragrance and provide a delicious subtle flavor that is fruitier than the heady perfumes of lavender and rose. Elder trees like their feet wet, so they are common along river banks and in ditches. The flowers grow in large bunches, which makes them very easy to harvest. Make sure you only harvest about 10 percent of each tree (see page 5) as elderberries are an important early source of food for birds and critters.

Elderflowers are most often used to make syrup that can be used in cocktails, drinks and baking. The dried flowers make an excellent tea.

· ·

ELDERFLOWER
BELLINI FIZZ
(page 41)

ELDERFLOWER
PROFITEROLE
(page 42)

ELDERFLOWER
FIG TART (page 37)

Figs represent abundance, sweetness and decadence. They rarely show up in my rural small-town grocery store but when they do, it's such a thrill! I had a fig tree in my backyard when I was growing up in Africa. I would wait impatiently for the figs to swell and ripen in the summer. I love their velvety mouthfeel, subtle flavor and lingering sweetness. Adding them to any recipe moves it from the mundane to the sublime.

Elderflower Fig Tart

To make the crust, sift the flour, sugar and salt into a bowl. Using your fingertips, rub in the butter until the mixture resembles bread crumbs. Add the water a tablespoon at a time until there is just enough to bring the dough together. Be careful not to overwork the dough. Turn out the dough, shape it into a disk, cover it in plastic wrap and refrigerate for 20 minutes.

Grease and flour a 9-inch (23 cm) tart pan.

On a lightly floured surface, roll out the dough to an 11-inch (28 cm) circle, then carefully transfer it to the tart pan. Gently work it into the edges and up the sides of the pan, and trim off the excess. Using a fork, prick the bottom of the dough all over, cover the surface directly with plastic wrap and refrigerate until needed.

Preheat the oven to 325°F (160°C).

continues

MAKES ONE 9-INCH (23 CM) TART

FOR THE CRUST

2¼ cups (550 ml) all-purpose flour

¼ cup (60 ml) granulated sugar

Pinch coarse kosher salt

1 cup (250 ml) unsalted butter, cold and cut into cubes

3 Tbsp (45 ml) cold water

To make the filling, sift the almond flour, icing sugar, cornstarch and all-purpose flour into a bowl.

Using a stand mixer fitted with the paddle attachment, cream the butter, salt, vanilla and almond extracts on medium speed for 2 minutes until light and fluffy. Scrape down the sides and bottom of the bowl and add the flour mixture. Beat on medium speed just until incorporated, about 1 minute. Scrape down the sides and bottom of the bowl again. Add the egg, beating until just mixed, about 1 minute.

Remove the pie crust from the fridge and pour the filling into it. Spread the filling evenly over the crust and bake until golden brown, about 40 minutes. Remove the tart from the oven and drizzle the simple syrup over the warm tart. Place the tart pan on a wire rack and let cool completely.

Spread the fig jam evenly over the top of the cooled tart.

Wash and dry the figs and remove the stems. Cut the figs into slices and arrange on top of the tart.

Store the tart in an airtight container in the fridge for 2–3 days.

FOR THE FILLING

⅔ cup (150 ml) almond flour

¾ cup (175 ml) icing sugar, sifted

¾ tsp (4 ml) cornstarch

1 tsp (5 ml) all-purpose flour

⅓ cup (75 ml) unsalted butter

Pinch coarse kosher salt

½ tsp (2 ml) pure vanilla extract

¼ tsp (1 ml) almond extract

1 extra-large egg, beaten

2 Tbsp Elderflower Simple Syrup (page 40)

½ cup (125 ml) fig jam

1 lb (450 g) fresh figs

Baking cakes should never be an activity reserved for special occasions. You should bake a cake because your snowdrops bloomed, for friends who have done nothing to deserve it and because it's Tuesday. As cakes go, this is an especially wonderful one. I hope you bake it often!

. . . .

Lemon Elderflower Cake

Preheat the oven to 350°F (175°C). Grease and flour two 9-inch (23 cm) round cake pans.

To make the cake, sift the flour and baking powder into a bowl.

Using a stand mixer fitted with the paddle attachment, cream the butter and sugar on high speed until light and fluffy, about 3 minutes. Mix in the lemon zest and simple syrup. Add the eggs one at a time, beating well after each addition.

Slowly add the flour mixture to the butter mixture, mixing on medium speed until just combined, about 3 minutes. Once the batter is combined, pour it into the prepared cake pans.

Bake until a skewer inserted into the center of each cake comes out clean, 25–30 minutes. Place the cake pans on a wire rack. Leave the cakes for 10 minutes, then carefully turn them out onto the wire rack to cool completely.

To make the frosting, using a stand mixer fitted with the paddle attachment, cream the butter with the icing sugar and simple syrup on high speed until light and fluffy, about 10 minutes.

Place one cake layer on a cake stand and top it with about one-third of the frosting. Sandwich the second layer on top. Now use the remaining frosting to frost the outside of the cake. Decorate with fresh edible flowers.

Store the cake in an airtight container in the fridge for 3–4 days.

MAKES ONE DOUBLE-LAYER 9-INCH (23 CM) CAKE

Photo on page 43

FOR THE CAKE

1¾ cup (425 ml) all-purpose flour

2 tsp (10 ml) baking powder

1 cup (250 ml) salted butter, at room temperature

1 cup (250 ml) superfine sugar

Zest of 2 lemons

2 tsp (10 ml) Elderflower Simple Syrup (page 40)

4 large eggs

FOR THE FROSTING

½ cup (125 ml) salted butter, room temperature

2 cups (500 ml) icing sugar, sifted

2 Tbsp (30 ml) Elderflower Simple Syrup (page 40)

Fresh edible flowers, for decorating

This syrup is a wonderful addition to cocktails, and, when added to club soda, makes a refreshing summer drink.

Elderflower Simple Syrup

Put the boiling water in a large heatproof bowl, add the elderflower blossoms and leave to steep for 2 hours or overnight.

Strain out the flowers, but don't squeeze them or the syrup will be bitter. Pour the elderflower water into a large pot and bring to a boil over medium heat. Add the sugar and stir until dissolved, about 5 minutes. Leave to cool.

Store the syrup in an airtight container in the fridge for 1 month.

MAKES 2 CUPS (500 ML)
Photo on page 103

4 cups (1 L) boiling water
4 cups (1 L) elderflower blossoms, washed and dried (see page 34)
4 cups (1 L) granulated sugar

TIPS: Add a couple of teaspoons of the elderflower simple syrup to transport your gin and tonics to dizzying heights.

You can make a delicious elderflower drink by diluting 1 part syrup to 3 parts water or soda water.

I only drink prosecco on two occasions: when it's my birthday and when it isn't. All the flower syrups in this book make excellent additions to a celebratory glass of prosecco, but elderflower is the best.

. . . .

Elderflower Bellini Fizz

Fill a tall glass with ice and pour the elderflower syrup overtop. Add the prosecco and club soda, give it all a quick stir and garnish with a lemon twist.

TIPS: Make a lemon twist by cutting a very thin slice of lemon peel with a vegetable peeler. Using a sharp paring knife, slice the peel into narrow strips. Twist a strip of peel into a corkscrew shape.

You can make elderflower gin to enjoy throughout the summer months. Pop 13 washed and dried flower heads into a very large clean mason jar, add 4 cups (1 L) of gin and 2 Tbsp (30 ml) of granulated sugar. Give it a good stir and leave it for three days. Give it a jiggle twice a day to encourage the sugar to dissolve. Strain out the flowers, but don't squeeze them or your drink will be bitter. Discard the flowers and enjoy the best damn G&T of the summer! Store in an airtight container.

SERVES 1

Photo on page 36

Ice cubes

¼ cup (60 ml) Elderflower
  Simple Syrup (page 40)

3 oz (75 ml) prosecco

2 Tbsp (30 ml) club soda

Lemon twist (see tip)

Choux pastry takes some serious elbow grease to make, but it's a small price to pay for a delicious treat like profiteroles. Besides, all this mixing will mean you get to eat more pastries once they're done!

Elderflower Profiteroles

Preheat the oven to 400°F (200°C). Line 2 large baking sheets with parchment paper.

Place the butter, water and salt in a medium pot and bring to a boil over medium heat. Add the flour and stir energetically and constantly until a sticky dough forms, about 5 minutes. Transfer the dough to a stand mixer fitted with the paddle attachment, and mix on medium speed for 5 more minutes. The dough should look like a thick paste.

With the mixer running on medium, add the eggs one at a time, beating well after each addition. The dough should be smooth, glossy and firm enough to hold its shape.

Transfer the dough to a piping bag fitted with a large, round tip. Pipe rounds about 1½ inches (4 cm) wide onto the prepared baking sheets. Wet a finger and gently press down the peaks left by the piping bag.

Bake until puffy and golden brown, 20–25 minutes. Place the baking pans on wire racks and let cool.

Place the cream, simple syrup and icing sugar in a medium bowl and whip until stiff. Transfer the cream to a clean piping bag fitted with a large round tip.

Slice the cooled choux buns in half horizontally with a serrated knife. Pipe a dollop of cream on the bottom half and replace the top.

Using a double boiler or a bowl set over a pot of simmering water, melt the chocolate chips. Spoon the melted chocolate over the profiteroles and serve to your adoring fans!

MAKES 40–48
PROFITEROLES

½ cup (125 ml) salted butter

1 cup (250 ml) water

Pinch coarse kosher salt

1 cup (250 ml) all-purpose flour

4 large eggs

2 cups (500 ml) whipping (35%) cream

1 tsp (5 ml) Elderflower Simple Syrup (page 40)

½ cup (125 ml) icing sugar

1 cup (250 ml) semisweet chocolate chips

TIP: To fill a piping bag (or plastic freezer bag with the corner cut), twist the bag just behind the tip and tilt the tip up so your filling won't leak out. Lower the upturned tip into a large beer glass so that the bag is resting securely in the glass. Now fold the top of the bag over the edges of the glass. That way you can fill it with no mess. Once you've filled the bag, unfold the bag from the glass and tie it off with an elastic band or use a bag sealing ring. Remove the piping bag from the glass and untwist the tip to use.

LEMON ELDERFLOWER
CAKE (page 39)

ELDERFLOWER
PROFITEROLES (page 42)

4.

4. GENUS: *VIOLA ODORATA*   **PERENNIAL**

· ·

IDENTIFICATION:

Violets have dark green, heart-shaped leaves with gently jagged edges. Their sweet little purple (or white or yellow) flowers have a distinctive five-petal pattern. Pansies have a similar but not identical leaf structure and five-petal flower pattern, and they come in a wide variety of colors and sizes.

Violets have two of their flower petals pointing up and the remaining three pointing down. Pansies have four petals turned up and only one pointing down. Both are edible and you can use either in every recipe in this section.

GROWING:

Violets are very easy to grow and will tolerate a wide variety of soils, although they prefer rich, moist, well-drained soil in partial shade. They will also grow in full sun and can be planted in early spring or grown from seed in garden beds. Violets will self-seed, and so you'll find their sweet little faces popping up all over the garden, but I've never minded that myself.

Violets only flower in the spring, but pansies bloom from early spring well into the fall. Pansies are surprisingly frost-resistant and will keep on cheerfully flowering as long as you deadhead them regularly.

Pansies in pots need to be watered almost daily. Pansies will tell you they need water by wilting a little, but they bounce back as soon as you give them a drink. You can also touch the soil around the roots and, if it's dry, give the pansies a good soak.

Pansies produce little seed pods that are star-shaped when they are open. I leave a few flowers in the fall, rather than deadheading them all, so I can collect seeds for the next growing season.

Wild Violets

Pansies and violets both belong to the genus *Viola*. While most of us use the terms interchangeably, there are subtle differences in their appearance. I use both violets and pansies in my spring and summer dishes. I love the happy little faces of violets and pansies and plant them all over my garden and in tubs on the porch. In addition to cooking and baking with them, I add them to salads, decorate cakes with them, press them for winter projects and candy them for kicks. After picking the flowers, shake out any bugs, then rinse and pat dry with a paper towel or leave out to dry.

These sweet little rolls are a healthier alternative to fried spring rolls. Play around with the fresh ingredients to find the flavor combo you love best. I've used pansies here as they have a fresh, subtle taste, but feel free to use other flowers too. Nasturtiums will add a spicy kick, while marigolds will add a sour edge. The peanut dipping sauce is my favorite part, but you can serve them with a sweet chili sauce too.

Pansy Fresh Spring Rolls

To make the rolls, place the green onions, carrots, mango, cabbage, basil and cilantro in a medium bowl and mix to combine.

Dip a wrapper in a pie plate filled with lukewarm water for 15 seconds and lay it on a plate carefully so it doesn't stick to itself. Place ⅛ of the pansies in a row down the center. Add ⅛ of the rice noodles and then ⅛ of the veggies and ⅛ of the shrimp, if you're using them. Fold up the bottom of the wrapper and stick it down on the sides. Fold down the top and stick it to the sides. Wrap the left side over the filling, then wrap the right side over the top, pressing gently to ensure it all sticks together.

To make the dipping sauce, mix together all the ingredients in a small bowl and serve on the side.

SERVES 8

FOR THE ROLLS

4 green onions, julienned

1 carrot, grated

1 mango, julienned

½ purple cabbage, thinly sliced

½ cup (125 ml) basil leaves

½ cup (125 ml) cilantro leaves

8 rice-paper wrappers

1 cup (250 ml) pansies, washed and dried (see page 45), stems removed

1 (8.8 oz/250 g) package rice noodles, cooked

1 cup (250 ml) cooked shrimp, optional

FOR THE DIPPING SAUCE

½ cup (125 ml) creamy peanut butter

1-inch (2.5 cm) piece fresh ginger, peeled and finely chopped

¼ cup (60 ml) water

1 Tbsp (15 ml) honey

1 tsp (5 ml) rice vinegar

1 tsp (5 ml) soy sauce

ULTRA VIOLET
COCKTAIL
(page 53)

PANSY FRESH SPRING
ROLLS (page 46)

DANDELION SALAD
WITH VINAIGRETTE
(page 10)

PEONY JAM
(page 58)

DANDELION
JAM
(page 16)

HIBISCUS JELLY
(page 185)

VIOLET
JELLY
(page 49)

NASTURTIUM
JELLY (page 146)

These ain't your grandma's violets! With their unbelievable pop of color, violets make a stunning jelly. The color can be steeped from the flowers by making a simple tea. When you soak the flowers in hot water, the water turns a dark blue. Add an acid (like lemon juice) and it turns the most incredible magenta. The change is so dramatic that violets served as litmus testers for early scientists. It's a great parlor trick to have up your sleeve.

Violet Jelly

Put the water in a large heatproof bowl, add the violet flowers and leave to steep for at least 2 hours (overnight is better) to make violet tea. Strain out the flowers, but don't squeeze them or your jelly will be bitter. Discard the flowers.

Prepare your jars for canning by boiling them in a canning pot for 10 minutes. Using long tongs or a jar lifter, transfer the jars to a wire rack and allow to cool.

Place the violet tea in a large pot and mix in the lemon juice and pectin. Bring to a rolling boil over high heat and add the sugar all at once. Stir to help the sugar dissolve. Bring to a boil again, still at high heat, and stir for 1 minute until all the sugar has dissolved. Remove the pot from the stove. Scoop the froth off the top of the jelly and discard.

Spoon your jelly into your jars and seal the lids firmly. Check the water level in your canning pot, place the jars back into the pot and boil them for 10 minutes. Using long tongs or a jar lifter, transfer the jars to a wire rack to cool.

Store this jelly in the jars at room temperature for 1 year and for 1 month in the fridge after opening.

MAKES 5-6 CUPS
(1.25-1.5 L)

2½ cups (625 ml) boiling water

3 cups (750 ml) violet flowers,
  washed and dried (see page 45)

2 Tbsp (30 ml) freshly squeezed
  lemon juice

1 (1¾ oz/49 g) package
  powdered pectin

6 cups (1.5 L) granulated sugar

You don't need to buy a silicone mold to make these lollipops, but I suggest you do simply because they're so much fun! You don't need to restrict yourself to violets and pansies; any edible plants, flowers and fruit can be popped into a lolly. If you don't have a mold, you can dab a bit of the melted sugar mixture onto a piece of parchment paper, then add the flower and stick, and pour a little more melted sugar mixture on top.

Violet and Pansy Lollipops

Place the flowers between two pieces of paper towel. Squish them under a heavy cookbook while you prepare the lollipops.

Spray your molds (or parchment paper) with cooking spray.

Combine the sugar, water and corn syrup in a small pot and gently warm it over medium heat, stirring occasionally, until the mixture registers 300°F (150°C) on a candy thermometer. If you don't have a candy thermometer, you can drop a little of the mixture into a glass of cold water. If it balls up, it's ready!

Remove the pot from the heat and mix in the extract. Let the syrup cool slightly for 2 minutes so it doesn't shrivel the flowers.

Pour a little of the candy mixture into each lollipop mold. Carefully place a flower on top and add a stick, followed by a little more sugar mixture to finish it off. Leave to cool.

When the lollipops have cooled completely, remove them from the molds and use a paper towel to wipe off the grease from the cooking spray.

MAKES 14 LOLLIPOPS

14 violets, pansies or a combination, washed and dried (see page 45)
2 cups (500 ml) granulated sugar
1 cup (250 ml) water
½ cup (125 ml) corn syrup
2 tsp (10 ml) extract of your choice (I like peppermint, orange, vanilla or rose)
14 lollipop molds or sticks

TIPS: You can add a little food coloring to the mixture, but not too much or you won't see the flowers.

You can press dry flowers so you can make these in the winter too.

CANDIED VIOLETS AND
PANSIES (page 52)

VIOLET AND
PANSY
LOLLIPOPS
(page 50)

Candied violets and pansies are an exercise in patience. I sit in the shade of my sugar maple in the summertime, delicately painting the petals and dipping them, which I find marvelously meditative. I dry them and store them in sealed bags for when I am making cakes or need a little something special to add to a dessert. They are so magical and, massive bonus, they taste great too.

. . . .

Candied Violets and Pansies

I like to squish the clean violets and pansies under a large cookbook before I start so that they will lie flat. Dip a soft paintbrush in the egg white and paint it on the petals.

Dip the flowers in the sugar and gently shake off any excess. Place on a parchment-lined baking tray and leave in a sunny place to dry.

Store the candied flowers in an airtight container in a cool, dry place for up to 1 year.

MAKES 24 CANDIED FLOWERS
Photo on page 51

24 violets or pansies or a
   combination, washed and
   dried (see page 45)
1 egg white, lightly beaten
¼ cup (60 ml) superfine sugar

Nothing adds color to cooking quite like violets. Keep this syrup a vibrant blue or add a little lemon for the most vivacious magenta. Either way, this syrup will add pizzazz to your cocktails, pancakes and ice creams. It can be frozen as a granita.

Violet Simple Syrup

Put the boiling water in a large nonreactive heatproof bowl, add the violet blossoms and leave to steep for 2 hours or overnight to make violet tea.

Strain out the flowers, but don't squeeze them or the syrup will have a bitter aftertaste. Discard the flowers.

Add 1 tsp (5 mL) of the lemon juice to the violet water, if using. Continue adding 1 tsp (5 mL) at a time until the desired color is achieved. Pour the water into a large pot and bring to a boil over high heat. Add the sugar and stir until dissolved, about 2 minutes.

Store the syrup in an airtight container in the fridge for 1 month.

MAKES 5 CUPS (1.25 L)

Photo on page 102

4 cups (1 L) boiling water

4 cups (1 L) violets, washed
  and dried (see page 45)

1 Tbsp (15 ml) freshly squeezed
  lemon juice (omit if you want
  blue syrup)

4 cups (1 L) granulated sugar

TIPS: Add a couple teaspoons of syrup to vodka and soda or gin and tonic to add a lovely color, or make a delicious violet drink by diluting 1 part syrup to 3 parts water or soda.

Well, this doesn't suck! A gorgeous spring cocktail that tastes as good as it looks.

Ultra Violet Cocktail

Fill a cocktail shaker half full with ice. Add the rum, lime juice and violet syrup. Shake, strain and serve with a garnish of fresh violets.

SERVES 1

Photo on page 47

Ice cubes

3 fl oz (80 mL) Cuban white rum

2 Tbsp + 2 tsp (40 mL) freshly
  squeezed lime juice

4 tsp (20 mL) Violet Simple
  Syrup (see above)

Fresh violets, washed and dried
  (see page 45), for garnish

5.

5. GENUS: *PAEONIA*   PERENNIAL

. . . .

IDENTIFICATION:

Peonies come in two varieties: garden peonies (*Paeonia valbiflora*) and tree peonies (*Paeonia suffruticosa*) which have filamented leaves as well as woody stems that don't die back in the winter.

Garden peonies come in many varieties. Single garden peonies have big fat petals in a single whorl around very impressive stamens in the center of the flower. Garden peonies also come in semi-double and double varieties with multiple feathery-edged petaloids within the center of the flower. These are mixed in with the stamens. The leaves of garden peonies are dark green and shiny with smooth edges, giving a lush tropical look through the growing season after the flowers have gone.

GROWING:

Peony tubers should be planted in the fall in full sun, although peonies can tolerate a little shade. Fertilize them well in the spring when the first foliage appears and support the plant with a peony cage so the blooms don't droop (no one likes droopy blooms!). Space your peony tubers 35–47 inches (90–120 cm) apart. Set peony roots into the soil at a depth of about 1–2 inches (2–5 cm), making sure the eyes are facing the skies. Peonies love fertile, humus-rich, moist soil that has a neutral pH and drains well.

When your plants grow too big, they will start to flower less. When that happens, it's time to divide the tubers. Make sure to do this in the fall after the foliage has died down.

Water peonies at the root every week. Peony foliage can be prone to mildew, especially if the plant lacks air circulation or you are watering the upper part of the plant rather than the soil. If you catch mildew early as a white or gray coating on stems and leaves, snip off the affected branches at ground level and dispose of them in the garbage, not the compost. Don't leave mildewed stems lying on the soil as they are a contaminant. After picking the flowers, shake out any bugs, then rinse and pat dry with a paper towel or leave out to dry.

Peonies

I shouldn't pick a favorite flower—it would be like picking a favorite child—but if I *had* to, it would be peonies. I love these outrageous blooms with a delicate fragrance and an even more delightful taste—a subtle floral mix of peach and strawberry. Peonies symbolize bashfulness and beauty, and *damn*, are they romantic! Their flowering season is fleeting, and they don't last long once you pick them, but their ephemerality is what I love most about them. You really do have to stop and smell the peonies. Your life will be so much more pleasant for having taken the time to do so.

LAVENDER CLAFOUTIS
(page 98)

DUTCH BABY
(page 21)

LATTICE PANCAKES
WITH CHANTILLY CREAM
(page 69)

CRUMPETS
WITH
PEONY JAM
(page 59)

As soon as their peonies start to drop their petals in a wild tantrum, my neighbors swoop in and collect them for me. Bags and bags of fragrant peony petals start showing up on my back porch. They are all lovingly shaken out to give the bugs a chance to escape, then rinsed and gently dried with a dish towel. I use some for this beautiful jam and freeze the rest so we can immerse ourselves in the sweet peony scents of summer in the depths of winter. The petals freeze beautifully, and you can use exactly the same amount of frozen petals as you do fresh to make this jam. To freeze, store rinsed and patted dry petals in a resealable freezer bag for up to 3 months.

Peony Jam

Put the water in a large heatproof bowl, add the peony petals and leave to steep for 2 hours or overnight to make peony tea. Strain out the petals, but don't squeeze them or your jam will be bitter. Discard the petals.

Prepare your jars and lids for canning by boiling them in a canning pot for 10 minutes. Using long tongs or a jar lifter, transfer the jars to a wire rack and allow to cool.

Place the peony tea in a large pot and mix in the lemon juice and pectin. Bring to a rolling boil over high heat and add the sugar all at once, stirring to dissolve. Bring to a boil again, still over high heat, stirring constantly. Boil for 1 minute and then remove from the heat. Gently tear the extra peony petals into strips and mix into the jam. Scoop the froth off the top of the jam and discard.

Spoon your jam into your jars and seal the lids firmly. Check the water level in your canning pot, place the jars back in the pot and boil for 10 minutes. Using long tongs or a jar lifter, transfer the jars to a wire rack to cool.

Store this jam in the jars at room temperature for 1 year and for 1 month in the fridge after opening.

MAKES 5–6 CUPS (1.25–1.5 L)
Photo on page 48

4 cups (1 L) boiling water

1 cup (250 ml) fresh peony petals, washed and dried (see page 54), plus extra for decorating

1 tsp (5 ml) freshly squeezed lemon juice

1 (1¾ oz/49 g) package powdered pectin

4 cups (1 L) granulated sugar

TIPS: The jam color will depend entirely on the color of the petals you used. If you only have white and light pink, feel free to add a few drops of natural food coloring to your jam.

Don't want to use so much sugar? Use diabetic pectin and cut down the sugar to 1–2 cups (250–500 ml) depending on taste. This pectin will ensure the jam sets properly.

Traditional crumpets are made with yeast and cooked on one side only on a griddle in special crumpet rings, leaving the top pitted. My crumpets are more like mini pancakes. They are easier to make and are the perfect vehicle for jam, fresh cream and loads of butter. Yum!

. . . .

Crumpets with Peony Jam

Using a stand mixer fitted with the paddle attachment, mix the flour, baking powder, eggs, vanilla, sugar, milk, salt and melted butter on medium speed for 2 minutes.

Heat your oven to 170°F (75°C) or turn on your warming drawer.

Warm a large nonstick pan over low heat, and lightly grease it with vegetable oil. Drop a tablespoonful of the batter onto the pan. Cook on one side until bubbles form on the top, about 1 minute, then flip it over and cook for 30 seconds on the other side.

Once the crumpets are ready, you can keep them toasty and warm in the oven until you're ready to eat. Continue making crumpets until the batter is finished.

Butter the crumpets while they are hot, then add a layer of peony jam and a dollop of whipped cream.

MAKES 18–20 CRUMPETS

Photo on page 57

1 cup (250 ml) all-purpose flour

1 tsp (5 ml) baking powder

2 large eggs

1 tsp (5 ml) pure vanilla extract

¼ cup (60 ml) granulated sugar

½ cup (125 ml) whole milk

Pinch table salt

2 tsp (10 ml) melted unsalted butter

TOPPINGS

¼ cup (60 ml) salted butter, or more to taste

Peony Jam (page 58)

Whipped cream

LOVESICK MARTINI
(page 63)

ZA'ATAR EGGPLANT
CRISPS WITH
AIOLI (page 79)

PEONY AND BRIE
APPETIZER
(page 61)

Jam and cheese baked in a pie? So much better than four and twenty blackbirds! During the 17th century, royal chefs tried to outdo each other with pies made in exciting shapes like manor houses and strange beasts. Made with hot water crusts, the pies were free-standing and didn't need a pie dish. When the strange shapes became passé, one court chef placed live blackbirds in a baked pie crust. When the pie was opened, the birds escaped, to much delight. This started the trend of the surprise pie, which saw increasingly bizarre things emerging from pies. During the reign of King Charles I of England, for example, a chef for the Duke of Burgundy created a huge pie filled with musicians and a girl who popped out when the pie was opened. The surprise in this particular pie is the marriage of cheese, jam and pie crust, which makes for a wonderful creamy, crusty appetizer.

Peony and Brie Appetizer

Combine the flour, sugar, baking powder and salt in a medium bowl. Using your fingertips, rub in the shortening until the mixture resembles fine breadcrumbs. Add the water, a tablespoon (15 ml) at a time, to bring the dough together, being careful not to overwork it. Turn the dough out, shape it into a disk, cover it with plastic wrap and refrigerate for 20 minutes.

Preheat the oven to 400°F (200°C). Lightly grease a baking sheet.

Spread the peony jam evenly over the top of the brie right to the edges. Sprinkle the thyme and black pepper evenly over the jam.

continues

SERVES 6–8

2 cups (500 ml) all-purpose
   flour, plus extra for dusting
2 Tbsp (30 ml) granulated sugar
1 tsp (5 ml) baking powder
½ tsp (2 ml) fine kosher salt
⅓ cup (75 ml) vegetable
   shortening
6 Tbsp (90 ml) water
⅓ cup (75 ml) Peony Jam
   (page 58)
8 oz (225 g) brie cheese
1 Tbsp (15 ml) chopped fresh
   thyme leaves
Pinch freshly ground
   black pepper
1 medium egg, beaten
Crackers or crostini, for serving

On a lightly floured surface, roll out the pastry into a circle ⅛-inch (0.25 cm) thick and twice the diameter of the brie. Place the brie in the center, jam side down. Fold the pastry up and over the brie. Trim off any excess and secure the edges by pasting them down with the beaten egg. Turn the brie over and place it on the prepared baking sheet.

Roll out the pastry offcuts and cut three strips, each 12 inches (30 cm) long and ¼ inch (0.5 cm) wide. Fold them into one long braid. Brush the outside of the pastry with the remaining egg. Place the braid around the edge of the brie. Trim the excess and brush the braid with the egg mixture.

Bake until golden brown, about 30–35 minutes. Serve slightly cooled brie with crackers or crostini.

Peony simple syrup is a delightfully delicate addition to your mixology repertoire!

. . . .

Peony Simple Syrup

Place the boiling water in a large heatproof bowl, add the peony petals and leave to steep for at least 1 hour (overnight is better) to make peony tea. Strain out the petals, but don't squeeze them or your syrup will have a bitter aftertaste. Discard the petals.

Place the peony tea and the sugar in a medium pot and bring to a boil over medium heat. Boil, stirring occasionally until all the sugar is dissolved, about 5 minutes. Leave to cool.

Store the simple syrup in an airtight container in the fridge for up to 1 month.

MAKES 5 CUPS (1.25 L)
Photo on page 102

1 cup (250 ml) boiling water
1 cup (250 ml) peony petals, washed and dried (see page 54)
1 cup (250 ml) granulated sugar

TIPS: Add a couple teaspoons to your gin and tonic, vodka and soda and prosecco for a delicate floral note, or dilute 1 part syrup with 4 parts water or soda for a refreshing pop alternative. You can also pour it over your ice cream and pancakes.

Whether you like yours shaken or stirred, there's no drink that can match the pizzazz of the martini. Using vodka allows the delicate fragrance and taste of the peony to sing lead, while the cranberry provides the backing vocals.

. . . .

Lovesick Martini

Fill a cocktail shaker with ice. Add the vodka, cranberry juice, peony simple syrup and lemon juice. Shake well, then strain into a chilled cocktail glass. Serve with a fresh peony petal if desired.

SERVES 1
Photo on page 60

1½ oz (45 ml) vodka
3 Tbsp (45 ml) cranberry juice
1 Tbsp (15 ml) Peony Simple Syrup (see above)
1 Tbsp (15 ml) freshly squeezed lemon juice
1 peony petal, washed and dried (see page 54), optional

6. GENUS: *TYPHA*   PERENNIAL

. . . .

IDENTIFICATION:

Cattails have long, pale green, sword-shaped leaves that are between ½-inch and ¾-inch (1.25–2 cm) wide. Male and female flowers grow on the same stem, with the males at the top and the females at the bottom. The male flowers are covered in a beautiful, silky yellow pollen which is released and blown in the wind to neighboring flowers where it fertilizes the female bloom. Once its pollen has been released, the male flower withers away. If the female flower is pollinated, it forms the characteristic brown furry seed spike that can contain up to 200,000 seeds. This spike lasts all winter and then disintegrates into tiny seeds in the spring.

For cooking, it's the pollen of the male flower that we are after. It is delicious, can be used as a substitute for flour and is high in protein. It's not just the pollen that's edible, though. Before they are fertilized, the female flowers are green and can be cooked and enjoyed with butter and salt, or pickled like cucumbers. The young spring leaf shoots can also be boiled, grilled or roasted and enjoyed as you would asparagus.

GROWING:

Cattails like full to partial sun and very moist conditions and can be found readily in the wild. You can easily harvest their pollen by gently shaking the male flowers over a paper bag.

You can replant cattail rhizomes or hand-sow the seeds. Cattails can grow in up to 12 inches (30 cm) of water and will need to be watered during droughts. Ensure that their soil always remains damp. Fertilize cattails in early spring when the new shoots first appear. Store harvested pollen in an airtight container for up to a year.

Cattails

One of the very first flowers to bloom as the weather warms is the cattail. Cattails emerge from creeping rhizomes that grow in muddy or marshy areas. Rhizomes are root stems that grow underground and send out roots.

Cattails represent peace, and a gift of cattail flowers is meant as a request to bury the hatchet. Failing that, the spikes make really fun swords. I once saw a kid accidentally take a bite of a cattail fruit he was holding, thinking it was a corndog. Lessons were learned.

. . . .

CATTAIL POLLEN TOMATO
GALETTE (page 67)

Galettes are gateway pies. There's no complex lattice pattern, crimping of the edges or blind baking. This is free-form pie at its finest—just roll the pastry out willy-nilly, throw in whatever you have in the fridge (sweet or savory) and chuck it in the oven. They make great lunches, superb starters and even better desserts. In this recipe, the earthy flavor of the cattails really helps to round out the tanginess of the tomatoes—a match made in heaven.

. . . .

Cattail Pollen Tomato Galette

To make the dough, place the flour, cattail pollen and salt in a large bowl and mix to combine. Using your fingertips, rub in the shortening until the mixture resembles breadcrumbs. Mix in the vinegar and just enough water (adding a tablespoon at a time) to form a soft dough. Be careful not to overwork the dough. Turn out the dough, shape it into a disk, cover in plastic wrap and refrigerate for 30 minutes.

Preheat the oven to 400°F (200°C).

To make the filling, slice the tomatoes lengthwise. Place the oil in a saucepan and warm it over medium heat. Lay the tomatoes in the pan, cut side down, avoiding overlapping. Fry until they start to brown on the edges, about 4 minutes.

On a lightly floured surface, roll out the dough to a 12-inch (30 cm) circle. You will be turning the edges in, but this is a free-form pie, so don't worry about making a perfect circle. Lay the tomatoes in the center, avoiding overlapping, and scatter the sugar, salt and pepper overtop. Fold the edges up over the filling, leaving the center of the pie exposed. Brush the folded-over pie dough with the egg yolk.

Bake until the pastry is golden brown, 25–30 minutes.

continues

SERVES 6

FOR THE DOUGH

1 cup (250 ml) all-purpose flour

⅓ cup (75 ml) cattail pollen
   (see tip)

½ tsp (2 ml) table salt

½ cup (125 ml) vegetable
   shortening, chilled, cut in cubes

½ tsp (2 ml) white vinegar

Cold water

FOR THE FILLING

2 cups (500 ml) mixed-color
   cherry tomatoes

1 Tbsp (15 ml) extra virgin olive oil

1 tsp (5 ml) granulated sugar

Pinch table salt

Pinch freshly ground black pepper

1 medium egg yolk, lightly beaten

10 fresh basil leaves

1 Tbsp (15 ml) chopped chives

Balsamic reduction (see tip)

Remove from the oven and let cool for 5 minutes. Garnish with fresh basil leaves and chives. Serve with the balsamic reduction on the side.

Store the galette in an airtight container in the fridge for up to 3 days.

TIPS: You can use ⅓ cup (75 ml) all-purpose flour if you don't have cattail pollen. The flavor will be less earthy, but still delicious.

Can you crumble feta cheese over the top as well? You can and you should!

You can buy a balsamic reduction or make your own. Simply place 2 cups (500 ml) of balsamic vinegar and ¼ cup (60 ml) packed brown sugar (optional) into a medium pot over medium heat. Simmer gently, stirring occasionally, until it's thick enough to coat the back of a spoon, 10–15 minutes.

Store leftover reduction in an airtight container in the fridge for up to a year.

Lattice pancakes are delicate and fun and neatly sidestep the stodginess of a classic stack. These pancakes will give the more artistic among you the opportunity to create food art of the highest order. Family portraits, renditions of your favorite postmodern pieces or just some squiggles in a pan will all taste equally good with a dollop of Chantilly cream.

. . . .

Lattice Pancakes with Chantilly Cream

Place the flour, pollen, sugar, baking powder, salt, egg, milk and butter in a bowl and mix until there are no lumps. Pour the batter into a sealable plastic bag or piping bag.

Heat your oven to 170°F (75°C) or turn on your warming drawer.

Cut the corner off when you are ready to make the pancakes so you can slowly squeeze the batter out. Keep a cup handy to rest the bag in between pancakes. Make one pancake at a time. Heat a lightly oiled nonstick pan over medium low heat. Squeeze 2 Tbsp (30 ml) of batter into the pan in a pattern (you can be as creative as you like). Cook until light golden brown, 45 seconds to 1 minute. Carefully flip and cook the other side for 30 seconds.

Once the pancakes are ready, you can keep them toasty and warm in the oven until you're ready to eat. Continue making pancakes until the batter is finished.

Using a stand mixer fitted with the whisk attachment, whip the cream, vanilla and sugar until stiff peaks form, about 3-4 minutes.

Drizzle the pancakes with maple syrup and smother in cream. Best enjoyed on the day they are made.

SERVES 4

Photo on page 57

FOR THE PANCAKES

1½ cups (375 ml) all-purpose
   flour
½ cup (125 ml) cattail pollen
   (see tip)
¼ cup (60 ml) granulated sugar
1 Tbsp (15 ml) baking powder
½ tsp (2 ml) table salt
1 large egg
1¼ cups (300 ml) whole milk
¼ cup (60 ml) unsalted butter,
   melted
Vegetable oil, for frying

FOR THE CHANTILLY CREAM

2 cups (500 ml) cold whipping
   (35%) cream
1 tsp (5 ml) pure vanilla extract
2 Tbsp (30 ml) granulated sugar
Maple syrup, to serve

TIP: Substitute all-purpose flour if cattail pollen is out of season.

LOVESICK
MARTINI
(page 63)

ALMOND CATTAIL
HEDGEHOG COOKIES
(page 72)

HIBISCUS
PB&J COOKIES
(page 191)

LAVENDER SHORTBREAD
COOKIES (page 99)

CHAMOMILE
MACARONS
(page 32)

Hedgehogs are one of my favorite woodland creatures. They're friendly, they're exceptionally good swimmers and climbers and they're immune to snake venom. The almonds in this recipe add a delightfully nutty taste that complements the earthiness of the cattail pollen perfectly.

· ·

Almond Cattail Hedgehog Cookies

Grease a large baking sheet or line with parchment paper.

Sift the flour, pollen, cornstarch, cinnamon, nutmeg and baking powder into a bowl.

Using a stand mixer fitted with the paddle attachment, beat the butter with the sugar on medium speed until light and fluffy, about 5 minutes. Add the egg and beat until well mixed, about 2 minutes. Add the almond and vanilla extract and mix well, about 2 minutes. Scrape down the sides and bottom of the bowl as needed.

Add the flour mixture to the butter mixture and mix on medium high to combine. Scrape down the sides and bottom of the bowl as needed. The dough should be soft, but not sticky.

Take a tablespoon (15 ml) of dough and roll it into a ball. The dough should not stick to your hands. If it's too wet, your hedgehogs will not keep their shape. Add a tablespoon (15 ml) of flour to the dough if it's too sticky. Pinch one end of the ball to make a nose and place on the prepared baking sheet. Push the sliced almonds into the ball to form quills. Make sure you press them in firmly or they'll fall out during baking. When the tray is full, place the cookies in the fridge for 15 minutes. This is essential if you want your hedgehogs to keep their shape.

MAKES 35–40 COOKIES

Photo on page 70

2½ cups (625 ml) all-purpose flour (see tip)

½ cup (125 ml) cattail pollen (see tip)

¼ cup (60 ml) cornstarch

2½ tsp (12 ml) ground cinnamon

Pinch ground nutmeg

1 tsp (5 ml) baking powder

1 cup (250 ml) salted butter, at room temperature, cut into cubes

1 cup (250 ml) granulated sugar

1 large egg

2 tsp (10 ml) almond extract

1 tsp (5 ml) pure vanilla extract

½ cup (125 ml) sliced almonds (see tip)

1 Tbsp (15 mL) black and white frostings or an edible pen, for decorating

Preheat the oven to 375°F (190°C).

Bake the cookies on the middle rack until the bottoms begin to brown, 10–12 minutes. Place the baking sheet on a wire rack and let the cookies cool completely.

Once the cookies are completely cool, use black and white frostings, chocolate or an edible pen to make the eyes and nose.

Store the cookies in an airtight container on the counter for up to 5 days, or in a sealed freezer bag in the freezer for up to 3 months.

TIPS: Cattail pollen is seasonal, so you can substitute all-purpose flour or almond flour for the cattail pollen.

The almonds toast gently in the oven and add a delicious texture and taste. They are time-consuming to place though, so if you prefer, you can toast the almonds and mix them in to the dough, but you won't get the thrill of the quill!

7.

7. GENUS: *RHUS*

PERENNIAL

· ·

IDENTIFICATION:

Sumac is a stunning tree that gives us not only a beautiful spice but also a vivacious fall display and gorgeous red berry spikes that provide color even in the dead of winter.

The trees belong to the Anacardiaceae family (a.k.a. the cashew or sumac family) and grow to between 3 and 33 feet (1–10 meters) tall. They have long, dark green rows of compound leaves on a yellow stem like a fern's leaf. Each leaf is oval with very jagged edges. You probably won't notice the very small, greenish, creamy white flowers with five petals, but when they fruit into red spikes at the end of the branch, they are quite striking.

GROWING:

Sumacs grow in well-drained soil and full sun. They grow from seeds spread by birds and by rhizomes that can cause great colonies of sumacs to grow in one area. To avoid colonizing your garden with sumac, grow it in an area where the perimeter of the sumac stand can be consistently mowed, or in container on a bright sunny patio in a growing medium that includes plenty of gravel and sand. Keep your container in a protected area over the winter.

Sumac

Sumac is a spice that provides a tart, lemony zing to many dishes. You can dry your own sumac for spice. Pick the fresh 'flowers' (clusters of drupes or berries) late in the spring when they are a deep red color. Break off the individual drupes and leave to dry in a warm, dry place for a day or two. When ready, rub your drupes through a sieve so the seeds stay behind. You want to remove the red hairs around the berry. Picking the drupes in early spring means there are more fine hairs, so they have a better taste and more vibrant color. As the summer progresses, you can still harvest the drupes, but you'll have to use more to get the same flavor. You can dry the spice on a parchment-lined baking sheet in a dry place for two days. Store it in an airtight container at room temperature for up to a year.

TAKE NOTE: There is a poison sumac with leaves and fruit that contain urushiol, which, like poison ivy, can cause skin irritations. However, this sumac produces whitish-gray, flattened fruit, so it would be difficult to mistake its fruits for the bright red edible kind.

. . . .

As the heat of summer sets in, all the tomatoes in my veggie garden seem to ripen at once, at two o' clock on a Tuesday. There are so many delightful ways to eat them, they never go to waste. Elevate your garden-variety tomato soup with the sourness of sumac and the creaminess of yogurt. The grilled cheese croutons are what really do it for me!

Sumac Tomato Soup with Grilled Cheese Croutons

Preheat the oven to 400°F (200°C).

To make the soup, place the tomatoes, onion and garlic on a baking sheet. Sprinkle the thyme and sumac over the veggies. Drizzle with the oil and then mix everything together until the vegetables are well coated.

Roast until the tomatoes begin to caramelize and the onions are soft, 25–30 minutes. Remove from the oven and transfer the tomato mixture to a large soup pot. Use an immersion blender to cream the veggies.

Mix in the broth and bring to a gentle boil, then simmer on low for 15 minutes. Stir frequently. Taste your soup and season to taste with sea salt and pepper.

To make the grilled cheese croutons, place 1 Tbsp (15 ml) of the butter in a frying pan and melt over low heat. Place 2 slices of bread in the pan and fry gently one side only until they start to brown, about 1 minute. Remove them from the pan. Place 1 cup (250 ml) of the cheese on the browned side of 1 slice and top with the other slice, browned side down. Melt another 1 Tbsp (15 ml) butter in the pan and cook the sandwich on both sides over low heat until brown, about 2 minutes per side. Repeat for the other sandwich. Cut the crust off your grilled cheese sandwiches and cut into small squares to make croutons.

Serve the soup with a dollop of plain yogurt and a garnish of grilled cheese croutons and fresh basil.

SERVES 4

FOR THE SOUP

3 lb (1.4 kg) ripe tomatoes, halved

½ large red onion, thinly sliced

3 cloves garlic

2 tsp (10 ml) fresh thyme leaves, or 1 tsp (5 ml) dried

1 tsp (5 ml) dried sumac (see page 75)

⅓ cup (75 ml) extra virgin olive oil

4 cups (1 L) vegetable broth

Sea salt and freshly ground black pepper, to taste

1 cup (250 ml) plain 3.5% yogurt, for serving

¼ cup (60 ml) chopped fresh basil leaves

FOR THE CROUTONS

¼ cup (60 ml) salted butter, divided

4 slices of your favorite crusty bread

2 cups (500 ml) grated cheddar cheese

TIPS: Don't want to make grilled cheese? Chop some halloumi into small squares and fry in butter until brown to use as croutons instead.

SUMAC TOMATO SOUP
WITH GRILLED CHEESE
CROUTONS (page 76)

Za'atar is a super-versatile Middle Eastern spice blend. It makes a perfect rub for chicken, beef, lamb or fish and a great addition to hummus and baba ghanoush; and you can mix it with olive oil to make a marinade or to use as a dip for crusty fresh bread.

. . . .

Za'atar Spice Mix

Place the cumin, coriander and sesame seeds in a small pan and toast over medium heat until dark and fragrant, 3–4 minutes. Remove the seeds from the heat and grind them in a blender or with a mortar and pestle. Mix the ground spices with the thyme, oregano, sumac and chili, if using.

Store the za'atar in an airtight container at room temperature for up to 1 year.

MAKES 80 G (2.8 OZ)

1 Tbsp (15 ml) cumin seeds

1 Tbsp (15 ml) coriander seeds

1 Tbsp (15 ml) sesame seeds

1 Tbsp (15 ml) dried thyme

1 Tbsp (15 ml) dried oregano

1 Tbsp (15 ml) dried sumac
  (see page 75)

1 tsp (5 ml) chili flakes
  (optional)

This is the best way to eat eggplant, if you ask me. Even your veggie-shy kids will love eggplant crisps! They are a wonderful snack on their own, as an appetizer or as a super side dish. The complex flavor profile of the za'atar spice mix shifts them from meh to marvelous.

. . . .

Za'atar Eggplant Crisps with Aioli

Preheat the oven to 425°F (220°C) and grease a baking sheet.

To make the eggplant crisps, peel the eggplant and cut it into paper-thin rounds (a mandolin works well for this, but you can use a very sharp knife).

Place the panko, Parmesan, za'atar, salt and cayenne pepper in a bowl and mix well to combine. Place the flour in another bowl and the beaten eggs in a third bowl.

Dredge the eggplant slices in the flour, then the eggs and then into the panko mixture, shaking off any excess from each bowl. Place on the baking sheet, being careful not to let them overlap.

Bake until golden brown, about 15 minutes, flipping them halfway through cooking time. Remove from the oven and let cool on the baking sheet for 10 minutes.

To make the aioli, using a food processor fitted with the steel blade or an upright blender, blend the garlic, salt, za'atar, lemon zest and juice, and Dijon until smooth, about 2 minutes. Add the eggs and—with the food processor running—slowly add the olive oil and then the vegetable oil. Blend to form your aioli.

Now grab those crisps and DIP! Crisps are best eaten on the day they are made. Store any leftover aioli in an airtight container in the fridge for about 1 week.

SERVES 6

FOR THE EGGPLANT CRISPS

1 large Italian eggplant

¾ cup (175 ml) panko crumbs

3 Tbsp (45 ml) grated Parmesan cheese

2 Tbsp (30 ml) Za'atar Spice Mix (page 78 or store-bought)

1 tsp (5 ml) coarse kosher salt

Pinch cayenne pepper

½ cup (125 ml) all-purpose flour

2 medium eggs, beaten

FOR THE AIOLI

2 cloves garlic

1 tsp (5 ml) coarse kosher salt

1 tsp (5 ml) Za'atar Spice Mix (page 78 or store-bought)

1 tsp (5 ml) lemon zest

3 Tbsp (45 ml) freshly squeezed lemon juice (1–2 lemons)

½ tsp (2 ml) Dijon mustard

1 large egg

1 large egg yolk

½ cup (125 ml) extra virgin olive oil

½ cup (125 ml) vegetable oil

SUMAC BRAIDED
BREAD STICKS
(page 81)

HALLOUMI TOMATO SALAD
WITH ZA'ATAR DRESSING
(page 83)

Full disclosure: I have chosen to frequent restaurants based on the deliciousness of their breadsticks! The breadstick combines all the yumminess of bread in a convenient, portable form. I highly recommend spoiling your dinner by eating far too many of these.

. . . .

Sumac Braided Breadsticks

Place the milk, butter and sugar in a small pot and place over low heat. Stir until the butter is just melted and the sugar is dissolved. The mixtures should be warm, but not hot. Remove from the stove and mix in the yeast. Set aside until the yeast starts to foam, 5–10 minutes.

Transfer the milk to a stand mixer fitted with the paddle attachment. Add 1 cup (250 ml) of the flour, the thyme, sumac, salt, pepper and honey. Beat on medium speed until combined, about 3 minutes. Add the remaining 1 cup (250 ml) of flour and mix on medium speed to make a stiff dough. Scrape down the paddle and the bowl. Fit the stand mixer with the dough hook and knead the dough until it's soft and elastic, 2–3 minutes. The dough will start to pull away from the bowl when it's ready.

Alternatively, turn out the dough onto a lightly floured surface and knead it with your hands until it's soft and elastic, 8–10 minutes.

Place the dough in an oiled bowl and cover the bowl with plastic wrap or with a damp tea towel. Leave it in a warm place until doubled in size, about 2 hours.

Lightly grease a baking sheet.

continues

MAKES 8

¾ cup (175 ml) 2% milk

2 Tbsp (30 ml) salted butter

1 Tbsp (15 ml) granulated sugar

1 envelope (2¼ tsp/11 ml) active dry yeast

2 cups (500 ml) all-purpose flour, divided

1 Tbsp (15 ml) fresh thyme leaves, or 1 tsp (5 ml) dried

2 tsp (10 ml) dried sumac (see page 75)

¼ tsp (1 ml) table salt

¼ tsp (1 ml) freshly ground black pepper

2 tsp (10 ml) honey

1 medium egg white, lightly beaten

Punch down the dough and, on a lightly floured surface, roll it out into a 10 × 9-inch (25 × 23 cm) rectangle that's 1 inch (2.5 cm) thick. Cut it into 24 equal pieces (a pizza cutter works well here). Roll the pieces into long, thin dough snakes. Each braid will use 3 pieces of dough. Braid the dough into 8 bread sticks, pinching the ends together. Place the breadsticks on the prepared baking sheet. Cover them with plastic wrap or a damp tea towel and leave them in a warm place to double in size, about 30–45 minutes.

At around the 20-minute mark, preheat the oven to 350°F (175°C).

Brush the egg white over the tops of the breadsticks and bake until golden brown, 15–18 minutes. Remove from the oven and transfer to a cooling rack to cool completely.

Store in an airtight container at room temperature for up to 3 days.

Ah, squeaky cheese, how I love your amazing taste! Halloumi is delicious as is and even more delicious when toasted in a pan. Add it to fresh tomatoes and a za'atar vinaigrette, and you and salad will finally be BFFs.

Halloumi Tomato Salad with Za'atar Dressing

To make the salad, place the oil in a frying pan and warm it over medium heat. Place the slices of halloumi in the pan and fry on each side until nicely browned, about 3 minutes per side. Set aside and let cool completely.

In a large bowl, arrange the tomatoes and onions to your liking. Top with the halloumi and basil leaves.

To make the dressing, place the ingredients in a small jar and shake well. Pour over the salad just before serving. Best served immediately.

SERVES 6

Photo on page 80

FOR THE SALAD

2 Tbsp (30 ml) extra virgin olive oil

8 oz (225 g) block halloumi cheese, cut in ¼-inch-thick (½ cm) slices

2 lb (900 g) heirloom tomatoes, cut into wedges

½ small red onion, thinly sliced

10 fresh basil leaves

FOR THE DRESSING

½ cup (125 ml) extra virgin olive oil

¼ cup (60 ml) balsamic vinegar

2 Tbsp (30 ml) freshly squeezed lemon juice

2 cloves garlic, finely chopped

2 Tbsp (30 ml) Za'atar Spice Mix (page 78 or store-bought)

1 tsp (5 ml) coarse kosher salt

½ tsp (2 ml) freshly ground black pepper

BEEF AND SHIITAKE
PIE (page 85)

SUMMER SQUASH SALAD
(page 152)

When the cheerfulness of the festive season gives way to the deep, dark winter that is January and you feel like you may never see the grass again, it's time for pie, my friends. In this recipe, a warm hearty filling is enveloped in a flaky pie hug that will comfort you and make you feel cozy and warm from the inside out.

. . . .

Beef and Shiitake Pie

Season the beef with the salt and let it sit at room temperature for 30 minutes.

To make the filling, put the shiitake mushrooms in a bowl and cover with the boiling water. Leave to rehydrate for 30 minutes, then remove them from the water, discard the stems and slice finely.

Place the oil in a large pot or Dutch oven and warm it over medium heat. Working in batches, add the beef and brown on all sides, about 4–6 minutes. Remove the browned beef from the pot and set aside on a plate. Add the garlic and onions to the pot and cook, still over medium heat, until the onions are soft, about 3 minutes. Add more vegetable oil, if needed.

Mix in the celery, carrots and sumac and cook until the vegetables start to soften, about 6 minutes. Mix in the browned beef and sliced shiitake mushrooms and fry for 2 minutes.

Add the flour and stir until well mixed. Stirring continuously so the flour doesn't clump, slowly pour in the broth and wine. Bring to a gentle boil over medium high heat. Mix in the bay leaves, cover, turn down the heat to low and simmer gently until the beef is super soft, about 45 minutes.

continues

MAKES ONE 9-INCH (23 CM) PIE

FOR THE FILLING

2 lb (900 g) beef chuck, cubed

1 tsp (5 ml) coarse kosher salt

1 oz (28 g) dried shiitake
  mushrooms

1¼ cups (300 ml) boiling water

¼ cup (60 ml) vegetable oil

2 garlic cloves, finely chopped

1 yellow onion, finely chopped

1 celery stalk, finely chopped

1 carrot, grated

2 tsp (10 ml) dried sumac
  (see page 75)

2 Tbsp (30 ml) all-purpose flour

2 cups (500 ml) beef broth

1 cup (250 ml) dry red wine

2 bay leaves

Meanwhile, to make the crust, place the flour and salt in a large bowl and mix to combine. Using your fingertips, rub in the shortening until the mixture resembles bread crumbs. Add the vinegar and 1 Tbsp (15 ml) of cold water at a time so there's just enough to bring the dough together. Be careful not to overwork it. Turn out the dough, divide it into 2 evenly sized pieces, shape them into disks, cover them with plastic wrap and refrigerate until your filling is ready, at least 20 minutes.

Remove the lid from the pot and let the filling cook for another 10 minutes to reduce the liquid. Taste and adjust the salt if necessary. Discard the bay leaves. Transfer the filling to a bowl and leave to cool a little. Adding hot filling to your pastry will melt the butter and create the dreaded soggy bottom, while filling that is too cold won't adhere to the crust. A slightly warm filling is ideal.

Preheat the oven to 400°F (200°C). Grease a 9-inch (23 cm) pie dish.

On a lightly floured surface, roll out each piece of dough to an 11-inch (28 cm) circle. Carefully transfer 1 circle to the prepared pie dish. Gently work it into the edges and up the sides of the dish, and trim off the excess. Add the filling and place the second circle of dough on top. Trim off the excess pastry and crimp the edges of the pie to seal. Brush with the egg yolk.

Bake until golden brown, 30–35 minutes. Let pie cool for 10–15 minutes before serving.

Store leftover pie in sealed container in the fridge for up to 3 days.

FOR THE CRUST

1½ cups (375 ml) all-purpose flour

½ tsp (2 ml) fine kosher salt

½ cup (125 ml) cold vegetable shortening, cut into cubes

1 tsp (5 ml) white vinegar

¼ cup (60 ml) ice-cold water

1 medium egg yolk, beaten

This is comfort food with a capital "C." It's well balanced with umami from the broth, sourness from the sumac and a kick of spice from the sausages. The little dumplings soak up all the flavor of the stew and get plump and soft and delicious. The best way to check they are done is to taste one (or, you know, two . . . just to be sure).

. . . .

Spicy Sausage Cornbread Cobbler

Preheat the oven to 400°F (200°C).

To make the stew, place the oil in a Dutch oven or an oven-safe pot with a lid and warm it over medium heat. Add the sausages and fry until browned on all sides, about 4–6 minutes. Remove the sausages from the pot and set aside to cool. Add the garlic and onions to the pot and fry gently, still over medium heat, until the onions are translucent, about 5 minutes.

Slice the cooled sausages into 1-inch (2.5 cm) pieces. Add the sausage slices, potatoes, sumac, paprika and cinnamon to the pot and cook, stirring frequently, until the potatoes begin to soften, about 5 minutes. Place the cornstarch in a small bowl and add 1 Tbsp (15 ml) water. Mix the cornstarch into a paste until there are no lumps. Add another 1 Tbsp (15 ml) water and mix to make a slurry. Pour the slurry over the sausage mixture and stir well. Add the broth and mix well to combine.

continues

SERVES 8

FOR THE STEW

⅓ cup (75 ml) extra virgin olive oil

1 lb (450 g) spicy Italian sausages

2 cloves garlic, crushed

1 large yellow onion, sliced

3 cups (750 ml) diced, peeled yellow potatoes

1 tsp (5 ml) dried sumac (see page 75)

1 tsp (5 ml) smoked paprika

½ tsp (2 ml) ground cinnamon

1 Tbsp (15 ml) cornstarch

2 cups (500 ml) beef broth

To make the cornbread, sift the flour, baking powder and salt into a large bowl. Add the buttermilk, egg and butter, followed by the corn, and mix until just combined. These dumplings are lumpy, so don't overmix in an effort to get the dough smooth or they might turn out chewy.

Gently drop small spoonfuls of the cornbread dough on top of the stew, then cover the pot with a lid. Bake in the oven, covered, for 15 minutes. Remove the lid and check the liquid level. If necessary, add more water until the liquid covers the stew. Bake, uncovered, until the dumplings are cooked through, about 15 minutes. Remove from the oven and leave to cool for 10 minutes before serving. Garnish with the chives.

Store the cobbler in a sealed container in the fridge for up to 3 days.

FOR THE CORNBREAD

1½ cups (375 ml) all-purpose flour

2 tsp (10 ml) baking powder

½ tsp (2 ml) coarse kosher salt

1 cup (250 ml) full-fat buttermilk

1 large egg, lightly beaten

2 Tbsp (30 ml) salted butter, melted

2 cups (500 ml) fresh corn kernels, or frozen and thawed

2 Tbsp (30 ml) chopped chives

TIPS: Add ½ cup (125 mL) grated cheddar cheese to the dumpling dough if you like.

SPICY SAUSAGE CORNBREAD
COBBLER (page 87)

Sumac's sour bite gives this soup a whole lot of pizzazz. Like citrus, it lifts the flavor and brightens the dish. On a cold winter day, this sumac soup will put some pep in your step!

. . . .

Sumac Mushroom Soup

Wash the mushrooms, pat dry, then slice and set aside.

Place the oil in a soup pot or Dutch oven and warm over medium heat. Add the garlic and ginger and fry, stirring constantly, until fragrant, about 2 minutes. Add the red onions, chili and sumac and fry, stirring constantly, until onion is translucent, about 5 minutes. Add the mushrooms and cook until they begin to soften, about 2 more minutes. Mix in the broth, vinegar and soy sauce and bring to a boil over medium heat. Turn down heat to low and simmer, uncovered, stirring occasionally for 10 minutes. Taste the soup and adjust salt as needed. Garnish with the green onions and serve hot.

Store the soup in a sealed container in the fridge for up to 3 days.

SERVES 6

Photo on page 117

4 cups (1 L) mixed mushrooms (shiitakes, enoki and oyster mushrooms work well)

¼ cup (60 ml) extra virgin olive oil

3 cloves garlic, finely chopped

2-inch (5 cm) piece fresh ginger, peeled and finely grated

1 large red onion, diced

1 red chili, finely chopped (include seeds for a hotter result or discard for mild heat)

1 Tbsp (15 ml) dried homemade sumac (see page 75)

8 cups (2 L) vegetable broth

¼ cup (60 ml) rice vinegar or white vinegar

¼ cup (60 ml) soy sauce

4 green onions, thinly sliced

Lemonade is a wonderful way to showcase the delicate, lemony deliciousness of sumac that can get lost when you use it as a spice. This lemonade is best in the spring, just when the sumac clusters have turned a deep red. The small hairs on the sumac are where the flavors are the most concentrated. They can be knocked off by wind and rain as the summer progresses.

Foraged Sumac Lemonade

Put the sumac clusters in a large bowl. Smoosh them with your hands, breaking the drupes (berries) off the stalk. You're trying to dislodge the hairs on the sumac through agitation. Pour in the water and steep overnight.

Strain out and discard the sumac drupes. Transfer the sumac water to an 8 cup (2 L) serving jug. Sweeten your lemonade with honey if you wish. Chill and serve on its own or as a cocktail mixer.

Store sumac lemonade in the fridge for up to 5 days.

SERVES 8

3 large sumac clusters
  (see page 75)
8 cups (2 L) boiling water
Honey, to taste (optional)

8.

8. GENUS: *LAVANDULA ANGUSTIFOLIA*   PERENNIAL

IDENTIFICATION:

Lavender bushes grow up to
3 feet (just under 1 meter) tall
and produce gray foliage and
purple flowers. Some varieties
have pink, blue or white flowers.
Lavender are part of the genus
Lamiaceae which includes
47 species of the mint family.

TIP: When you're drying your
lavender, don't make the bunches
too big or they will develop mold.

GROWING:

Lavandula angustifolia is otherwise known as old English
lavender and can be planted as a perennial, even up to
zone 5 in a protected area. *Lavandula x intermedia* is
a different kind of lavender and is grown as an annual,
often in containers.

My farm is in zone 5 and I grow armfuls of lavender.
I grow old English, Provence, Hidcote, Munstead and
Phenomenal lavender varieties for different reasons.
Choose the one that matches your needs and
climate zone.

Plant lavender in full sun in well-drained soil. It doesn't
need a lot of water, so water mature plants every
2 weeks. Give it a light "haircut" prune at the end of
the growing season. Pruning the green section of the
stems will rejuvenate your plants but avoid cutting into
the woody structure which could damage your plant.

Lavender

There are more varieties of lavender than you can shake a sharp stick at. Note that lavender has the ability to make your food taste incredible or soapy, depending on which type you use. It's best to stick to the *Lavandula angustifolia* varieties. They won't make your shortbread take like grandma's hand soap. There are over 100 varieties of *Lavandula angustifolia*, so you're sure to find one that grows well in your zone.

CULINARY LAVENDER: Creating your own culinary lavender could not be easier. Pick the lavender when the buds are still tightly wrapped. Don't leave it until the flowers open or they won't dry as well. Cut the lavender just above where the leaves begin to grow on the stem. Shake out the flowers to ensure any bugs are freed. Gather the blooms into bundles about 2 inches (5 cm) in diameter, and hang upside down in a dark, cool place. Leave to dry for 7 to 10 days.

Once dry, run your finger along the stem to remove the buds. Place them in a food processor and process until finely powdered, about 2 minutes. Store in an airtight container at room temperature for up to 3 years.

. . . .

This is a stew for cold, rainy days or days when the snow is flying and you need a meal that is as comfy as a PJs-and-movie night. This will stick to your ribs, leaving you full and satisfied for hours!

. . . .

Guinness Beef Stew

Season the beef with the salt and let it sit at room temperature for 30 minutes.

Place 2 Tbsp (30 ml) of the oil in a stewing pot or Dutch oven and warm it over medium heat. Working in batches, add the beef and brown on all sides. Remove the browned beef from the pot and set aside on a plate.

Add the remaining 2 Tbsp (30 ml) oil to the pot and warm over low heat. Add the onions and fry until translucent, about 5 minutes. Mix in the garlic, herbes de Provence and pepper. Fry for 2 minutes, still on low heat, until fragrant. Mix in the bacon, carrots and celery, and fry until the bacon begins to crisp, about 4 minutes. If the herbs begin to stick, you can add another 1 Tbsp (15 ml) oil.

Place the cornstarch in small bowl and mix 2 Tbsp (30 ml) water. Mix well until there are no lumps. Add the remaining 2 Tbsp (30 ml) water and mix to form a slurry. Add the cornstarch slurry to the stew, mix well to combine and fry for 2 minutes over low heat, stirring constantly until it begins to thicken. Stir in the broth, beer, tomato paste and bay leaves.

Put the beef back into the pot and mix to combine all the ingredients. Bring to a boil, then reduce heat, cover and simmer very gently over low heat until meat is tender, about 2 hours. Check regularly and add more broth if the liquid gets low and the meat or veggies are sticking out. Uncover and cook for another 30 minutes to thicken the stew. Serve hot.

SERVES 6

Photo on page 97

2½ lb (1.125 kg) stewing beef, cubed

1 tsp (5 ml) coarse kosher salt

¼ cup (60 ml) extra virgin olive oil, divided

2 red onions, chopped

3 garlic cloves, finely chopped

2 Tbsp (30 ml) Herbes de Provence (page 104)

¾ tsp (4 ml) freshly ground black pepper

6 oz (180 g) bacon, diced

3 large carrots, diced

2 large celery stalks, cut into 1-inch (2.5 cm) pieces

2 Tbsp (30 ml) cornstarch

¼ cup (60 ml) water, divided

3 cups (750 ml) beef broth

1 (14.9 fl oz/440 mL) can Guinness beer

1 (5½ fl oz/156 mL) can tomato paste

3 bay leaves

Store any cooled leftover stew in an airtight container in the fridge for up to 3 days.

TIPS: To bulk this meal up even further, you can make dumplings and add them just before you pop the lid on the Dutch oven. To make dumplings, place 1 cup (250 ml) all-purpose flour, 2 tsp (10 ml) baking powder and ½ tsp (2 ml) coarse kosher salt in small bowl and mix to combine. Using your fingertips, rub in 1 Tbsp (15 ml) unsalted butter until the mixture resembles bread crumbs. Mix in ½ cup (125 ml) whole milk to form a dough. Roll the dough into balls and place them on top of the stew. They'll suck up a lot of moisture, so double the amount of broth you add to the stew and check on it regularly to ensure the stew doesn't dry out.

This stew is traditionally served with mashed potatoes, the addition of which makes it even heartier.

GUINNESS BEEF STEW
(page 94)

A clafoutis is essentially a baked batter containing fruit. It originates from Limousin, France. Once you've mastered the batter itself, feel free to use whatever seasonal fruits you have on hand for the filling. Larger berries like strawberries should be quartered.

Lavender Clafoutis

Preheat the oven to 425°F (220°C). Grease a 10-inch (25 cm) cast-iron skillet, at least 1¾ inches (4.5 cm) deep. If you don't have a cast-iron skillet, you can use a deep pie dish.

Place the blueberries in the prepared skillet.

Place the milk, eggs, butter, vanilla, sugar, lavender and salt in a large bowl and whisk to combine. Add the flour and whisk until completely smooth. Pour this batter over the blueberries.

Bake until the clafoutis is golden brown on top, 25–30 minutes. Place the skillet on a wire rack and let the clafouti cool slightly (it will deflate a bit). Serve warm, with a scoop of ice cream.

Store any leftover clafouti in an airtight container in the fridge for 2–3 days.

MAKES ONE 10-INCH
(25 CM) CLAFOUTIS
Photo on page 56

2 cups (500 ml) fresh
   blueberries, or any
   combination of berries
1 cup (250 ml) whole milk
3 large eggs
2 Tbsp (30 ml) salted butter,
   melted
1 tsp (5 ml) pure vanilla extract
½ cup (125 ml) granulated sugar
2 Tbsp (30 ml) dried, ground
   culinary lavender (see tips on
   page 93)
Pinch table salt
½ cup (125 ml) all-purpose flour
Ice cream, for serving

Traditional Scottish shortbread dates back to the 12th century. It's a wonderful reminder that simple is so often best.

. . . .

Lavender Shortbread Cookies

To make the shortbread, sift the flour into a small bowl and gently mix in the lavender.

Using a stand mixer fitted with the paddle attachment, cream the butter with the sugar on high speed until light and fluffy, about 3 minutes. Add the salt, vanilla and almond extracts and mix, still on high speed, until smooth and creamy, about 4 minutes.

Add the flour mixture to the butter mixture and mix on medium just until combined, about 3 minutes). The dough should be soft and crumbly. Turn out the dough, divide it into 2 evenly sized pieces, shape each piece into a disk, wrap them with plastic wrap and refrigerate for 1 hour, or up to overnight.

About 30 minutes before you're ready to bake, preheat the oven to 350°F (175°C).

On a lightly floured surface, roll out 1 piece of dough to about to ½-inch (1.25 cm) thickness, and then cut out cookies using a cookie cutter of your choosing. Re-roll and cut out any leftover dough for more cookies. Place them on an unlined baking sheet.

Bake until the cookies are just browned around the edges, 10–13 minutes. Place the cookies on wire racks and let cool completely. Repeat with the second piece of dough.

continues

MAKES 30–35 COOKIES

Photo on page 71

FOR THE SHORTBREAD

2 cups (500 ml) all-purpose flour

1 tsp (5 ml) dried, ground culinary lavender (see tips on page 93)

1 cup (250 ml) unsalted butter, at room temperature

¾ cup (175 ml) granulated sugar

½ tsp (2 ml) fine kosher salt

2 tsp (10 ml) pure vanilla extract

½ tsp (2 ml) almond extract

To make the icing, using a stand mixer fitted with the whisk attachment, whip all the icing ingredients on high speed until stiff peaks form, about 5 minutes. If you are adding color, scoop some of the icing out and mix with food coloring now. Transfer the icing to a piping bag (see tip, page 42) and decorate the cookies with your own designs.

Store the iced cookies in an airtight container at room temperature for up to 3 days.

ICING

3½ cups (875 ml) icing sugar, sifted

3 large egg whites

1 tsp (5 ml) freshly squeezed lemon juice

Food coloring (optional)

TIPS: Use the correct variety of lavender to ensure your shortbread is not soapy (see page 93).

Blitz the lavender in your processor or grind it up with a mortar and pestle so that it can be evenly distributed through the dough.

Lavender syrup is a great addition to cocktails and summer drinks or enjoy it over pancakes and ice cream!

. . . .

Lavender Simple Syrup

MAKES 2 CUPS (500 ML)

Photo on page 102

Prepare your jars for canning by boiling them in a canning pot for 10 minutes. Using long tongs or a jar lifter, transfer the jars to a wire rack and allow to cool.

Place the lavender flowers, water and lemon juice in a small pot and bring to a boil over high heat. Add the sugar, stir to combine, turn down the heat to low and simmer gently, uncovered, stirring frequently, for 15 minutes.

Turn off the heat and let the syrup cool in the pot. Strain into prepared jars. Store the syrup in the fridge for 1 month.

TIP: This syrup is amber, so add purple coloring or beet powder while it's still in the pot to get a dazzling purple color that will make your cocktails pop.

3 Tbsp (45 ml) dried lavender flowers (see page 93)

1 cup (250 ml) water

¼ tsp (1 ml) freshly squeezed lemon juice

2 cups (500 ml) granulated sugar

TIP: To make a refreshing summer drink, dilute 1 part syrup with 4 parts water or soda water.

Lazy lavender summers start with this wonderful sweet treat. Lavender will add flavor and color to your favorite drinks, so it's a superb addition to your summer cocktail repertoire. It's rumored to reduce stress and keep bugs at bay, so it's the perfect drink for hammock hangs!

. . . .

Lavender Love Martini

SERVES 1

Photo on page 209

Fill a cocktail shaker with ice. Add the vodka, simple syrup and lemon juice and stir gently until mixed. Strain into a martini glass and garnish with a fresh sprig of lavender.

Ice cubes

2 oz (60 ml) vodka

2 Tbsp (30 ml) Lavender Simple Syrup (see above)

2 Tbsp (30 ml) freshly squeezed lemon juice

1 sprig fresh lavender, for garnish

LAVENDER
SIMPLE SYRUP
(page 101)

PEONY
SIMPLE SYRUP
(page 63)

VIOLET
SIMPLE SYRUP
(page 53)

ELDERFLOWER
SIMPLE SYRUP
(page 40)

ROSE
SIMPLE
SYRUP
(page 164)

DANDELION
WINE (page 11)

HIBISCUS
SIMPLE SYRUP
(page 184)

Channel your inner Victorian duchess with this lavish lavender recipe—it's fancy as heck! You can add lavender sugar to your cookies, muffins and crème brûlée for additional scrumptiousness, or to your evening tea to help get you to sleep. Try using it to line the rim of cocktail glasses or to sweeten your herbal teas. It pairs especially well with citrus teas.

Lavender Sugar

MAKES 2 CUPS (500 ML)

Mix the together the sugar and lavender in a bowl and transfer to an airtight container.

Store the sugar in an airtight container at room temperature for up to 2 years.

2 cups (500 ml) granulated sugar
1 Tbsp (15 ml) dried lavender
  flowers (see page 93)

You can use this superb general herb mix from southern France to flavor just about anything: chicken, veggies, fish, hearty stews . . . I was introduced to it through culinary legend Julia Child, from her book *Mastering the Art of French Cooking* in a recipe for poulet sauté aux herbes de Provence. If your cookbook library is missing this classic, get thee to a bookstore, my friend. You can, of course, buy this herb mixture, but it's super easy to make your own.

Herbes de Provence

MAKES ½ CUP PLUS 2 TBSP
(155 ML) SPICE MIX

Place the herbs in an airtight container and mix to combine.

Store the herbes de Provence in their airtight container in a cool, dry place for up to 3 months.

2½ Tbsp (37.5 ml) dried oregano
2½ Tbsp (37.5 ml) dried thyme
2 Tbsp (30 ml) dried savory
2 Tbsp (30 ml) dried, ground
  culinary lavender (see tips on
  page 93)
1 tsp (5 ml) dried basil
1 tsp (5 ml) dried sage
1 tsp (5 ml) dried rosemary

Sweet dreams are made of teas, and this blend will have you nodding off in no time. The calming chamomile and lavender will relax you while the valerian sends you off to sleep. Escape the toil and strife of the waking world by sipping this somnambulant blend and slipping into sweet, sweet oblivion.

· ·

Sleepy Time Tea

Place the herbs in a tea ball or in a teapot. Pour boiling water overtop and leave to steep for 3 minutes. Strain out the herbs and add vanilla and honey to taste. Discard the herbs.

TIP: Turn your tea into a latte and add the comfort of warm milk to your bedtime routine. Place the herbs in a small pot and pour in 1 cup (250 ml) of your preferred milk. Warm it over medium heat until hot but not boiling. Strain the milk into your favorite mug through a tea strainer to remove the herbs. Add vanilla and honey to taste and serve hot.

SERVES 1

1 Tbsp (15 ml) dried chamomile
   flowers (see page 18)

1 tsp (5 ml) dried rose petals
   (see page 148)

½ tsp (2 ml) dried lavender
   flowers (see page 93)

½ tsp (2 ml) valerian root
   (optional)

1 cup (250 ml) boiling water

½ tsp (2 ml) pure vanilla extract

Honey, to taste

9.

9. GENUS: *CENTAUREA CYANUS*   **ANNUAL**

· ·

IDENTIFICATION:

The stems and the leaves are long and pointed and a grayish green color. The composite flowers are made up of many small flowers with tattered fringe petals. The flowers appear in late June and will keep on going until the first fall frost.

GROWING:

Sow cornflower seeds after the last spring frost in rich, damp soil in full sun. They like well-drained soil and are vulnerable to rot if the soil is too damp. Cornflowers need about 1 inch (2.5 cm) of water each week. If you wish to see this annual again in the garden next year, deadhead the plant regularly through the summer, leaving the spent blooms in the beds. It should come up again on its own the following year.

You can pick the flower heads for use as a fresh ingredient in your dishes. You can dry the flowers by washing them and leaving them to dry on a paper towel for 4–6 days.

Cornflower

A member of the daisy family, the cornflower (aka bachelor's button, aka bluebottle) has the dreamiest blue color. It can also be found in pink, purple and white in wildflower seedling mixes. Cornflower petals are a bright and beautiful addition to any dish and can be dried for use in the winter.

In classical mythology, cornflowers are named after a melancholy boy named Cyanus, who loved blooms so much, he spent all his time weaving intricate flower wreaths. He wished more than anything to have a cloak the color of cornflowers. His longing consumed him and soon he was found dead in a field of cornflowers. The goddess Flora took pity on the boy for his obsession and transformed him into a cornflower, finally gifting him the blue coat he so desired.

Cornflowers represent the delicacy of hope of one whose love is cultivated forever. I can relate—I would happily spend all my days making wreaths of flowers in a field somewhere if I could.

· ·

CORNFLOWER BREAD
BOUQUET (page 109)

This is a delicious small-batch focaccia recipe that's a real crowd-pleaser. I mean, everyone loves getting flowers, but flowers wrapped in *bread*? Yes, please! Use fresh flowers in the summer and dried ones in the winter for equally stunning results.

. . . .

Cornflower Bread Bouquet

Preheat the oven to 400°F (200°C).

Place the room-temperature water and 2 Tbsp (30 ml) of the oil in small bowl. Add the rosemary, and set this herb oil aside while you make the dough.

Place the warm water in a small bowl. Sprinkle in the yeast and sugar, and leave until it begins to foam, 5–10 minutes.

Transfer the yeast mixture to a stand mixer fitted with a dough hook. Add the flour, salt and ¼ cup (60) of the oil and mix on medium speed until you have a sticky dough, about 5 minutes. Turn the dough out onto a lightly floured surface and, using your hands, knead it until it is no longer sticky, about 30 seconds. Place the dough in an oiled bowl, cover the bowl with plastic wrap or a damp tea towel and leave in a warm place to rise until doubled in size, 45–60 minutes.

Use the remaining oil to grease a 9½ × 6½-inch (23.5 × 16.5 cm) baking sheet. The pan should be well coated with oil.

Flour your hands and stretch the dough out to fit the pan. Slip the pan inside a large plastic bag and leave the dough to rise in a warm place for 30 minutes or until doubled in size.

continues

MAKES ONE 9 × 7-INCH
(23 × 18 CM) LOAF

1 Tbsp (15 ml) room-temperature
water

½ cup (125 ml) extra virgin
olive oil, divided

1 tsp (5 ml) chopped fresh
rosemary leaves (see tip)

¾ cup (175 ml) water, heated
to 110°F (45°C)

1 envelope (2¼ tsp/11 ml) active
dry yeast

1 tsp (5 ml) granulated sugar

2½ cups (625 ml) all-purpose
flour

1 tsp (5 ml) coarse kosher salt

¼ cup (60 ml) fresh cornflower
petals, washed and dried
(see page 106), or 2 Tbsp
(30 ml) dried

½ cup (125 ml) halved cherry
tomatoes

5 green onions, cut into thin
strips lengthwise

Coarse salt, for topping

Remove the plastic bag from the dough. Wet your hands and dimple the dough by sticking your fingers into it until you can feel the pan.

Pour the herb oil over the bread, using a pastry brush to evenly distribute the oil. Scatter the cornflower petals overtop, and use the cherry tomatoes and green onions to create stems and flowers of your bouquet. Sprinkle with coarse salt. Bake until golden brown, 18–20 minutes. Place the baking sheet on a wire rack and let the bread cool slightly before serving.

Store the bread in an airtight container at room temperature for 2–3 days.

TIPS: You can use dried rosemary if you don't have fresh, but reduce the quantity to ½ tsp (2 ml).

Use any kind of edible flowers and vegetables to create your bouquet—this bread is perfect for using up leftovers!

Traditional gazpacho recipes use bread to provide a thicker consistency, so when you have some day-old bread and you're not sure what to do with it, reach for this great summertime snack. It's the perfect recipe for that Tuesday in August when all your tomatoes ripen at the same time and you have *way* too many.

. . . .

Watermelon Prosecco Gazpacho

Place all the ingredients, except the cornflower petals and bread, in a blender and blend until smooth. Adjust the salt to taste.

Serve cold with crusty bread. Garnish each serving with cornflower petals.

Store the gazpacho in an airtight container in the fridge for up to 3 days.

SERVES 4–6

Photo on page 131

1 cup (250 ml) deseeded and chopped ripe tomatoes

3 cups (750 ml) deseeded and chopped watermelon

2 cups (500 ml) chopped strawberries

1 small red chili, deseeded and chopped

2 garlic cloves, crushed

½ cup (125 ml) extra virgin olive oil

1 tsp (5 ml) coarse kosher salt

½ tsp (2 ml) freshly ground black pepper

½ cup (125 ml) prosecco

2 Tbsp (30 ml) freshly squeezed lime juice (1–2 limes)

2 slices crusty white bread, torn into 1-inch (2.5 cm) pieces

¼ cup (60 ml) fresh cornflower petals, washed and dried (see page 106), plus extra for garnish

CORNFLOWER ARTISAN
BREAD (page 113)

This no-knead bread is great for beginner bread-makers, but you have to leave it to rise for 12 hours, so plan ahead. A word of warning: this bread's scraggly dough will look dodgy right up until you pull the finished loaf triumphantly out of the oven. Don't doubt your bread-making abilities—just have a little faith.

. . . .

Cornflower Artisan Bread

Sift the flour, salt and sugar into a large bowl and add the yeast. Pour in the warm water, add the cornflower petals and, using your hands, mix until a sticky dough forms, being careful not to overwork it.

Cover the bowl with plastic wrap and leave in a warm place for 12 hours until it doubles in size.

Cut a piece of parchment paper to fit the bottom of your Dutch oven. Set it aside. Do not place it in the Dutch oven at this point.

Preheat the oven to 450°F (230°C). Warm your Dutch oven in the oven while it comes to temperature.

Turn out the dough onto the parchment paper and shape it roughly into a ball. Do not knead or punch it down. It should be sticky, wobbly and bubbly on top.

Brush the top of the dough with the egg, garnish with extra cornflower petals and then quickly but carefully transfer it, still on the parchment paper, to the heated Dutch oven. Cover with the lid and bake for 30 minutes. Remove the lid and bake until the bread is golden brown and crusty, about 10 minutes. Turn the bread onto a cooling rack and let cool completely.

Store the bread in an airtight container at room temperature for 1–2 days.

MAKES ONE MEDIUM ROUND LOAF

3 cups (750 ml) all-purpose flour

1½ tsp (7 ml) coarse kosher salt

1 Tbsp (15 ml) granulated sugar

½ tsp (2 ml) active dry yeast

1½ cups (375 ml) water, heated to 110°F (43°C)

¼ cup (60 ml) fresh cornflower petals, washed and dried (see page 106), plus extra for decoration

1 large egg, lightly beaten

TIPS: If you don't have a Dutch oven, use a small, oven-safe metal pot with a tight-fitting lid.

Level up your bread with ½ cup (125 ml) dried fruit (raisin bread!), ½ cup (125 ml) seeds and nuts, 2 Tbsp (30 ml) chopped herbs or ½ cup (125 ml) shredded or crumbled cheese (YES!). Add these additional ingredients after you have sifted the dry ingredients together.

10.

. . . .

IDENTIFICATION:

Marigolds are bushy annuals that range from 6 to 35 inches (15–89 cm) tall. Their dark green, fern-like leaves are opposite with serrated edges. The flowers can be single, semi-double, or fully double in yellows, oranges, reds and combo colors.

GROWING:

You can plant the seeds indoors 6–8 weeks before the last frost is expected, or you can sow them directly into the ground after the last frost, 1 inch (2.5 cm) apart. Marigolds like well-drained soil and direct sun. They are pretty hardy, but water them lightly once a week for optimum health.

Deadheading the flowers will encourage blooming and give you a wealth of seeds for the next year. You can use the fresh petals for cooking and dry them for use in the winter months. To dry the petals, shake out the flowers to free any bugs. Gently wash and pat dry with a dish towel. Grip the flower stem (green part) firmly, then twist off the petals, leaving the seeds behind. Lay petals out on a paper towel in a dry place for 3–5 days.

Marigolds

Marigolds are just here to party! They symbolize happiness and energy. In Thailand and India, they are threaded into long garlands for use in religious ceremonies, weddings and other celebrations. In Mexico, they are most often found on graves during the Día de Muertos celebrations. These happy-go-lucky annuals are one of the easiest flowers to grow. They thrive in very harsh conditions, poor soil and sunny places and need very little care despite all the love they give.

The plant group "marigold" actually encompasses two different genera of plants from the daisy family (*Asteraceae*). They include species from both the genus *Calendula* and the genus *Tagetes*. You can substitute calendula in the same volume for any of the recipes in this section. Calendula petals are larger and longer and the flowers look more like daisies. Both calendula and marigold come in a wide variety of warm colors. They grow abundantly and produce a phenomenal volume of seeds that are easy to harvest and grow in the spring.

· ·

PUMPKIN AND MARIGOLD
BISQUE (page 118)

SUMAC MUSHROOM
SOUP (page 90)

CHAMOMILE CARROT
SOUP (page 20)

Bisques, with their creamy, dreamy deliciousness, perfectly capture the essential nature of comfort food. The smoothness of the soup is complemented with a little crunch from the roasted pumpkin seeds. And you can sop up the leftovers with a crusty bread such as Cornflower Artisan Bread (page 113).

. . . .

Pumpkin and Marigold Bisque

Preheat the oven to 400°F (200°C).

Cut the pumpkin in half and scoop out the seeds. If you'd like to use them for a crunchy topping, rinse them, pat them dry and set aside.

Cut the pumpkin into 2-inch (5 cm) slices. Coat each piece in the oil and place on a baking sheet. Roast until you can poke a fork in them without resistance, 25–30 minutes. Remove the pumpkin from the oven and set aside to cool enough to handle.

If you're using the pumpkin seeds, turn down the oven temperature to 350°F (175°C).

Place the pumpkin seeds on a clean baking sheet, coat in 2 Tbsp (30 ml) olive oil and bake until golden brown, 12–15 minutes, turning every 5 minutes to ensure they toast evenly.

SERVES 4-6

Photo on page 116

1 medium pumpkin or two small
    sugar pie pumpkins (see tip)

3 Tbsp (45 ml) extra virgin
    olive oil plus 2 Tbsp (30 ml)
    more if you are roasting
    pumpkin seeds

3 Tbsp (45 ml) salted butter

½ cup (125 ml) fresh marigold
    petals, washed and dried,
    seeds removed (see page 114),
    plus extra for garnish

2 garlic cloves, finely chopped

1 medium yellow onion, chopped

2-inch (5 cm) piece ginger,
    peeled and finely chopped

2 tsp (10 ml) chopped fresh sage
    leaves, or ½ tsp (2 ml) dried

¼ tsp (1 ml) ground cinnamon

3 cups (750 ml) chicken or
    vegetable broth

1 Tbsp (15 ml) freshly squeezed
    lemon juice

1 cup (250 ml) whipping (35%)
    cream

Place the butter in a large pot and melt it over medium heat. Mix in the marigold petals, garlic, onions, ginger, sage and cinnamon. Fry gently, still over medium heat, until the onions are soft, 5–7 minutes. Scrape the pumpkin out of its skin and add it to the onion mixture. Mix to combine and fry for 2 minutes. Mix in the broth and turn down the heat to low. Bring to the boil, then reduce the heat and simmer, covered, for 20 minutes.

Add the lemon juice. Remove from the heat and, using an immersion blender, blend until smooth. Mix in the cream, then portion into bowls and garnish with toasted pumpkin seeds and marigold petals.

TIP: Any variety of pumpkin works, but sugar pie is the best, if you ask me.

FLOWER PASTA
WITH MARIGOLD PESTO
(page 121)

Be warned: once you make fresh pasta, it's really difficult to go back to store-bought. It's incredibly easy, extremely satisfying and absolutely delicious. This flower pasta in particular is beautiful, and I encourage you to experiment with other edible flower petals. If the petals are large, chop them up or the two layers of pasta won't stick together. Note that you'll need a pasta machine for this recipe.

. . . .

Flower Pasta
with Marigold Pesto

To make the pasta, on a clean work surface, pile up the flour and salt, and carefully whisk to combine with a fork. Make a well in the center and place the eggs and oil in it. Using a fork, carefully beat the eggs, slowly drawing in flour from the edges until a shaggy dough forms. It's okay to get stuck in with your hands as soon as the eggs are incorporated if you prefer.

You can do the next step by hand or in a stand mixer.

If you're using your hands, knead the dough on your work surface until it's elastic and soft, 8–10 minutes.

If you're using a stand mixer, fit it with a dough hook and mix the dough on medium speed until elastic and smooth, about 3 minutes.

Turn out the dough, cover it with plastic wrap and leave it to rest on the countertop at room temperature for 30 minutes.

Divide the dough into 2 evenly sized pieces, leaving one half in the plastic. Run the first half through your pasta machine, taking care to fold the edges in so the dough comes out in a nice rectangle. Repeat until you have run the pasta through the thinnest setting.

continues

SERVES 4

FOR THE PASTA

2 cups (500 ml) "00" flour

½ tsp (2 ml) coarse kosher salt

3 large eggs

1½ tsp (7 ml) extra virgin
  olive oil

½ cup (125 ml) fresh marigold
  petals, washed and dried,
  seeds removed (see page 114),
  plus more for garnish

Lay the pasta out on a lightly floured work surface. Sprinkle the marigold petals evenly over the top.

Run the second half of the dough through the pasta machine just like you did with the first piece, going all the way to the thinnest setting. Place this pasta rectangle on top of the first one and press down gently. Run the double layer of pasta through the machine on a medium speed one last time. Now use your cutting attachment to make fettucine. Flour the pasta well so it doesn't stick when you cook it.

Fill a large pot with water as salty as the sea and bring it to a boil over high heat.

Meanwhile, to make the pesto, using a food processor fitted with the steel blade, blitz the basil, Parmesan, marigold petals and pine nuts until smooth. With the machine running, add the garlic, slowly drizzle in the oil and then blend for 1 minute. Taste the pesto and add salt and freshly ground black pepper to taste.

Once the water is at a rolling boil, drop your fettucine in. It should only take 1–2 minutes to cook through.

Serve the pasta hot with a drizzle of pesto and a couple of marigold petals to garnish.

FOR THE PESTO

2 cups (500 ml) fresh basil leaves (see tip)

½ cup (125 ml) grated Parmesan cheese

½ cup (125 ml) fresh marigold petals, washed and dried, seeds removed (see page 114), divided

⅓ cup (75 ml) pine nuts

3 cloves garlic, finely chopped

½ cup (125 ml) extra virgin olive oil

Table salt and freshly ground black pepper, to taste

TIP: If you prefer, you can swap out 1 cup (250 ml) of the basil for 1 cup (250 ml) of dandelion greens.

I lived on instant noodles when I was in university, so I owe a debt of gratitude to this fast food. Roasted instant noodles add a really wonderful crunchy element to salads. You'll soon be adding them to all your salads with wild abandon. It doesn't matter what flavor of noodles you use, as the second step in this recipe is to throw away the flavor package.

. . . .

Marigold Crispy Noodle Salad

Preheat the broiler to high.

To make the salad, discard the flavor package from the pack of noodles.

Break the noodles onto a baking sheet in 1-inch (2.5 cm) pieces, place the baking sheet on the middle rack of the oven and broil the noodles for 2 minutes. Give the baking sheet a shake and put the noodles back under the broiler until they just begin to brown, about 1 minute. Watch them carefully—they can burn in a second! Set aside to cool.

Place both cabbages, the carrots and cilantro in a large bowl and mix to combine.

To make the dressing, place the garlic, marigold petals, chili flakes, pepper, salt, oil, maple syrup, soy sauce, peanut butter and lemon juice in a small bowl. Mix together to combine. Add a tablespoon (15 ml) of water at a time until you have just enough water to reach the consistency you want. Pour the dressing over the salad and mix well. Sprinkle the crispy noodles overtop.

TIP: Don't like cilantro? Sub in the same volume of julienned green onions.

SERVES 6 AS A SIDE

FOR THE SALAD

2¼ oz package instant noodles

½ cup (125 ml) finely shredded purple cabbage

½ cup (125 ml) finely shredded green cabbage

½ cup (125 ml) julienned carrot

¼ cup (60 ml) chopped cilantro (see tip)

FOR THE DRESSING

3 cloves garlic, crushed

¼ cup (60 ml) fresh marigold petals, washed, dried and seeds removed (see page 114)

2 tsp (10 ml) red chili flakes

1 tsp (5 ml) freshly ground black pepper

Table salt, to taste

¼ cup (60 ml) sesame oil

¼ cup (60 ml) maple syrup

2 Tbsp (30 ml) light soy sauce

2 Tbsp (30 ml) smooth peanut butter

Juice of 1 lemon

Water

These cookies are delicious as is, but I love to ice them. Icing cookies brings a whole new level of zen to baking. I love taking the time to create little works of art that I know will be devoured in minutes!

Marigold Sugary Buttery Cookies

To prepare cookies, sift the flour, baking powder and salt into a bowl, whisk to combine and gently add the marigold petals.

Using a stand mixer fitted with the paddle attachment, beat the butter with the sugar on high speed until light and fluffy, about 5 minutes. Add the egg, vanilla and almond extracts and mix well to combine, about 2 minutes. Scrape down the bottom and sides of the bowl as needed. With the mixer running on low speed, slowly add the dry ingredients and mix until combined. Scrape down the bottom and sides of the bowl as needed again. The dough should be soft, but not sticky.

Turn the dough out, divide it into 2 evenly sized pieces, shape them into disks, cover them with plastic wrap and refrigerate for at least 1 hour, or up to overnight.

Preheat the oven to 350°F (175°C). Grease 2 baking sheets.

Roll out the dough to ¼-inch (0.5 cm) thick. Cut out the cookies with 2-inch (5cm) cookie cutters, place them on the greased baking sheets and refrigerate for 10 minutes. This will prevent the cookies from spreading. Re-roll dough and continue to cut out cookies until you've used all the dough. Bake until the edges start to brown, 11–12 minutes. You can bake both pans at once, with one on the top rack and one on the bottom rack, swapping halfway through baking time. Leave to cool on the pan for a few moments and then transfer to a wire rack to cool completely.

MAKES 32–40 COOKIES AND 4 CUPS (1L) OF ICING

Photo on page 127

FOR COOKIES

2¼ cups (550 ml) all-purpose flour

½ tsp (2 ml) baking powder

¼ tsp (1 ml) table salt

3 fresh marigold flowers, washed and dried, seeds removed (see page 114) (about 3 Tbsp/45 ml; see tip)

¾ cup (175 ml) unsalted butter, at room temperature

¾ cup (175 ml) granulated sugar

1 large egg, at room temperature

2 tsp (10 ml) pure vanilla extract

½ tsp (2 ml) almond extract

FOR ROYAL ICING

3 large egg whites, at room temperature

4 cups (1 L) icing sugar

A couple of drops of food coloring

Store the cookies in an airtight container for up to 3 days.

To prepare royal icing, use a stand mixer fitted with the whisk attachment, whip the egg whites on high speed until frothy. With the mixer running on high speed, slowly add the sugar, whipping until stiff, glossy peaks form, 5–7 minutes. Check the consistency of your icing by scooping up a spoonful and drizzling it back over the icing in the bowl. If it incorporates in 8–10 seconds, it's perfect for icing details and borders. For flooding, you want a thinner consistency that incorporates in 3–4 seconds. Use the thicker icing for borders first, then flood with the thinner icing. Add more icing sugar to thicken or a little water to thin your icing. Divide your icing into bowls and add food coloring 1 drop at a time, mixing between drops, until you get the right color. Transfer the icing to piping bags or it will dry out, then ice cookies to your heart's content!

TIP: When harvesting the petals, grab the flower tightly in one hand and twist the petals off rather than pulling them. This will ensure you get the petals only and not any seeds as well.

Cake is the "happily ever after" ending to a great meal, and since you are what you eat, let it be sweet! Go ahead . . . You deserve it!

. . . .

Orange and Marigold Loaf Cake

Preheat the oven to 350°F (175°C). Grease and flour a 9 × 5-inch (23 × 13 cm) loaf pan.

Using a stand mixer fitted with the paddle attachment, mix the eggs with the sugar on medium speed until lighter in color, about 3 minutes. Add the orange juice and zest, marigold petals, oil, sour cream and vanilla and mix well to combine, about 2 minutes. Scrape down the bottom and sides of the bowl as needed. Sift the flour and baking powder and add to the egg mixture. Mix well to combine, about 2 minutes. Once the batter is combined, pour it into the prepared loaf pan.

Bake until a skewer inserted into the center of the cake comes out clean, about 30 minutes.

Meanwhile, to make the syrup, place the sugar, bourbon and orange juice in a small pot and bring to a boil over medium heat. Boil for 1 minute, stirring occasionally, then set aside.

When you take the cake out of the oven, use your skewer to poke holes in it and pour the syrup over it while it's still hot.

Place the pan on a wire rack. Leave the cake to cool in the pan for 10 minutes, then carefully turn it out and place it syrup side up on a wire rack to cool completely.

To make the glaze, mix the icing sugar with the orange juice. Pour the glaze over the cake when it has cooled. Sprinkle the petals over the top as decoration.

Store the cake in an airtight container in the fridge for up to 3 days.

MAKES ONE 9 × 5-INCH
(23 × 13 CM) LOAF

FOR THE CAKE

3 large eggs

1 cup (250 ml) granulated sugar

3 Tbsp (45 ml) freshly squeezed orange juice

Zest of 1 orange

¼ cup (60 ml) fresh marigold petals, washed, dried and seeds removed (see page 114)

¼ cup (60 ml) vegetable oil

3 Tbsp (45 ml) full-fat sour cream

1 tsp (5 ml) pure vanilla extract

2 cups (500 ml) all-purpose flour

1 Tbsp (15 ml) baking powder

FOR THE SYRUP

¾ cup (175 ml) granulated sugar

2 oz (60 ml) bourbon

¼ cup (60 ml) freshly squeezed orange juice (1–2 oranges)

FOR THE GLAZE

1 cup (250 ml) icing sugar

3 Tbsp (45 ml) freshly squeezed orange juice

3 Tbsp (45 ml) fresh marigold petals, washed, dried and seeds removed (see page 114)

ORANGE
AND
MARIGOLD
LOAF CAKE
(page 126)

Nikki

MARIGOLD SUGARY
BUTTER COOKIES
(page 124)

11.

11. GENUS: *TROPAEOLUM MAJUS*   **ANNUALS**

. . . .

IDENTIFICATION:

Nasturtiums have bright red, orange or yellow five-petal flowers. These tend to hide under the leaves, so move the foliage aside when you're harvesting. They have a vine-like growing pattern with small tendrils that latch on to things. Their round, silvery-green leaves have white veins connecting in the center.

GROWING:

Sow the seeds indoors 2–4 weeks before the last frost is expected or directly into the garden after the threat of frost has passed. The seeds will sprout in 7–12 weeks or when the soil has warmed to 55°F–65°F (13°C–18°C). Leave 12 inches (30 cm) around each plant so they have space to grow.

Nasturtiums like acidic, well-drained soil and do well in full or partial sun. Water them once a week (but back off if the leaves yellow or turn pale) and check often for aphids. Should aphids raid your nasturtium patch, spraying with soapy water will send them packing. Use 1 Tbsp (15 ml) soap to a 1 cup (250 ml) water. Ladybugs eat aphids, so encourage these cute little bugs to nest in your garden. You can also sometimes find ladybugs for sale in the natural pest control section of your garden center.

Nasturtiums that grow in partial sun are less spicy than those in full sun. If you find the flavor overwhelming, pick the shaded blooms and leaves instead. After picking the flowers, shake out any bugs, then rinse and pat the flowers and leaves and dry with a paper towel or leave out to dry.

Nasturtiums

Nasturtiums are a great entry point into cooking with flowers. They are often part of store-bought salads and offer a welcome bit of color and flavor with their tangy spiciness. They are a symbol of victory and patriotism—warriors would wear nasturtiums that were gifted to them by young women after battle.

I love them for their peppery taste, which reminds me of radishes. They are beautiful, prolific and very easy to grow thanks to their natural insect-repellent qualities. You can eat the flowers or use them as beautifully bright garnishes. The leaves are just as useful. I love them fresh in salads or shredded on top of a pizza instead of arugula. You can wilt the leaves in a pan with fried garlic and onion as a wonderful green side dish. Even the seeds are edible (and delicious) when pickled and turned into capers. Nasturtiums are a jolly, versatile, bright and cheerful edition to your garden and your kitchen!

They say you don't make friends with salad, but the combination of nasturtium flowers and strawberries in this bright, summer salad will have you knee-deep in new pals in no time.

Nasturtium Strawberry Salad

To make the salad, place all the salad ingredients in a serving bowl and toss to mix.

To make the dressing, put the dressing ingredients in a mason jar and shake to mix.

Dress the salad just before serving.

TIPS: Use roasted pecans or walnuts halves instead of pumpkin seeds for the crunchy element if you prefer.

Store leftover salad dressing in a sealed container in the fridge for up to 1 week.

SERVES 6

FOR THE SALAD

4 cups (1 L) hulled and
  quartered strawberries
3 cups (750 ml) baby spinach
3 cups (750 ml) nasturtium
  flowers and leaves, mixed,
  washed and dried
  (see page 128)
¼ cup (60 ml) pumpkin seeds
  (see tip)
½ small red onion, thinly sliced
¾ cup (175 ml) crumbled
  feta cheese

FOR THE DRESSING

¼ cup (60 ml) balsamic vinegar
3 Tbsp (45 ml) extra virgin
  olive oil
2 Tbsp (30 ml) poppy seeds
1½ Tbsp (22 ml) honey
½ tsp (2 ml) Dijon mustard
½ tsp (2 ml) coarse kosher salt
Pinch freshly ground
  black pepper

WATERMELON
PROSECCO
GAZPACHO
(page 111)

NASTURTIUM
STRAWBERRY SALAD
(page 130)

TOFU FLOWER
BROTH
(page 133)

Eat dessert first

flowers will bring good fortune

This is a very simple recipe—just tofu and broth—but it's the tofu flower that steals the show. When you cut the tofu nice and thin, the "petals" will move like a sea anemone. It's mesmerizing and so pretty you won't want to eat it.

Tofu Flower Broth

Place the sesame oil in a soup pot and warm it over medium heat. Add the garlic and ginger and fry until fragrant, about 30 seconds. Mix in the onions and fry until soft, about 4 minutes. If they start to stick, turn down the heat a little and an additional 1 Tbsp (15 ml) of oil. Add the carrots, mushrooms and nasturtium leaves and flowers, mix gently to combine and cook until the leaves have wilted, about 5 minutes. Mix in both broths and the water, cover, turn down the heat to low and simmer gently for 1 hour. The broth should be clear.

Strain out the solids, leaving a clear broth. Taste the broth and add just enough soy sauce to balance the flavors.

Cut the tofu into 4 evenly sized squares. If you have a rectangular block of tofu, trim a little off to make a square or your flowers will be lopsided. Cut off the corners to make a rounded shape. Wet your knife before cutting, or the tofu will stick to the knife and break. Gently slice the tofu from one end to the other, taking care to slice only about halfway through. Make the slices as thin as you can without breaking the tofu. Next, rotate the tofu and repeat horizontally. Slide the knife under the tofu and gently lift it into the broth. Garnish with a nasturtium leaf.

Store the broth in an airtight container in the fridge for up to 3 days.

SERVES 4

2 Tbsp (30 ml) sesame oil

5 cloves garlic, crushed

2-inch (5 cm) piece fresh ginger, peeled and finely chopped

1 red onion, sliced

2 large carrots, sliced

2 cups (500 ml) sliced mushrooms (see tip)

1 cup (250 ml) shredded nasturtium leaves, washed and dried (see page 128), plus 4 leaves for garnish

1 cup (250 ml) nasturtium flowers, washed and dried (see page 128)

4 cups (1 L) chicken broth

2 cups (500 ml) beef broth

2 cups (500 ml) water

Soy sauce, to taste

14 oz block extra-firm tofu

TIP: I love using earthy-tasting mushrooms like morels or shiitakes here, but button mushrooms would work too.

NASTURTIUM
STAR TEAR-AND-SHARE
BREAD (page 136)

SAFFRON BEER
CHEESE DIP (page 199)

A bread haiku:

The smell of fresh bread

Is there anything better?

No, bake no mistake!

This nasturtium pesto bread is supposed to be for sharing, but you don't have to!

· ·

Nasturtium Star Tear-and-Share Bread

To make the bread, place the milk in a medium bowl and warm it in the microwave until lukewarm, about 15 seconds. Stir in the sugar and the yeast and set aside until foamy, 10–15 minutes.

Using a stand mixer fitted with the dough hook attachment, mix the yeast mixture, flour and egg yolks on high speed until a soft, silky dough forms, about 4 minutes. Add the butter 1 Tbsp (15 ml) at a time, mixing well between each addition. The dough should be soft and silky, but not sticky.

Oil the sides of a mixing bowl and place the dough in the bowl. Cover the bowl with plastic wrap or a damp tea towel and leave in a warm place until doubled in size, about 45 minutes.

Meanwhile, to make the pesto, place all the ingredients in a blender and blend until smooth. Divide into 3 equal parts.

Place a 10 × 10-inch (25 × 25 cm) piece of parchment paper on a work surface.

Knock the dough down and divide it into 4 evenly sized pieces.

SERVES 8–10

Photo on page 134

FOR THE BREAD

¾ cup (175 ml) whole milk

3 Tbsp (45 ml) granulated sugar

1 envelope (2¼ tsp/11 ml) active dry yeast

2⅓ cups (575 ml) all-purpose flour

2 large eggs, separated

¼ cup (60 ml) salted butter

FOR THE PESTO

½ cup (125 ml) fresh basil leaves

½ cup (125 ml) nasturtium leaves and flowers, washed and dried (see page 128)

1 clove garlic, finely chopped

¼ cup (60 ml) grated Parmigiano Reggiano cheese

1 Tbsp (15 ml) pine nuts, toasted (see tip)

½ cup (125 ml) extra virgin olive oil

On a lightly floured surface, roll out 1 piece of the dough into an 8-inch (20 cm) circle. Place it in the center of the parchment paper.

Coat the dough with 1 portion of the pesto, making sure you go right to the edges. Repeat the process with the next 2 dough pieces, stacking them on top of the first one. Roll the last one out and place it on top so it looks like a stack of pancakes. The last piece of dough has no pesto on it.

Turn a small glass upside down and place it in the center of the stack. Now make 4 straight, evenly spaced cuts in the dough circles, like wheel spokes, cutting all the way through the dough but taking care not to cut the dough under the glass. Make another 4 evenly spaced cuts so you have 8 pieces, and repeat so you have 16 evenly sized pieces in total, all still connected to the dough under the glass.

Pick up one of the pieces and turn it gently twice to the right. Pick up the next piece and turn it twice to the left. Go around the circle, alternating directions, until all the pieces are twisted. Remove the glass. Your dough should resemble a 16-legged spider.

Gently pick up the parchment and place it on a baking sheet or in a Dutch oven. Leave the bread in a warm place until doubled in size, about 45 minutes. You can cover it with a large plastic bag or a damp tea towel as long as they don't touch the dough.

Preheat the oven to 350°F (175°C).

Place the egg whites in a small bowl, gently beat them and then brush them over the bread.

Bake until golden brown, 15–20 minutes. Leave to cool for 10 minutes then serve warm.

Store the bread in an airtight container for up to 3 days.

TIP: Pine nuts are easy to toast. Simply pop them in a pan over medium heat (no oil needed). Cook, stirring constantly, until they are brown and fragrant, about 3 minutes. Immediately transfer from the pan to a plate to cool.

SPICY FISH TACOS
(page 139)

NASTURTIUM
CAPERS (page 142)

NASTURTIUM
HOT SAUCE (page 141)

My idea of a balanced diet is a taco in each hand. I love experimenting with taco fillings, and this is a really good one. The combination of spicy nasturtium leaves and flowers makes for a color and taste bomb that will have you coming back for thirds!

. . . .

Spicy Fish Tacos

To make tortillas, place the flour, salt and baking powder in a bowl and make a well in the center. Using your fingertips, rub in the shortening until the mixture resembles bread crumbs. Add 1 Tbsp (15 ml) water at a time until a shaggy dough forms. Turn the dough out onto a floured surface. Knead until soft, about 2 minutes. Divide the dough into 16 evenly sized balls. Press each ball down with your palm, place on an ungreased baking sheet, cover with a damp tea towel or plastic wrap and leave to rest in a warm spot for 15 minutes.

Preheat the oven to 375°F (190°C). Grease a baking sheet with olive oil.

Meanwhile, to make the dressing, place the sour cream, mayonnaise, lime juice and hot sauce in a small bowl and mix to combine.

To make the tacos, place the saffron, cumin and cayenne pepper in a small bowl. Mix in the salt and pepper.

Rub the spice mix on both sides of the fish and place the fish on the baking sheet. Dot each fillet with a piece of butter.

Bake until soft and flaky, 20–25 minutes.

continues

SERVES 4

FOR HOMEMADE TORTILLAS

3 cups (750 ml) all-purpose flour

1 tsp (5 ml) table salt

1 tsp (5 ml) baking powder

6 Tbsp (90 ml) vegetable shortening or lard, cut in cubes

1 cup (250 ml) water, heated to 110°F (45°C)

FOR THE DRESSING

½ cup (125 ml) full-fat sour cream

⅓ cup (75 ml) mayonnaise

2 Tbsp (30 ml) freshly squeezed lime juice

1 Tbsp (15 ml) Nasturtium Hot Sauce (page 141, or your favorite hot sauce; see tip)

Meanwhile, roll out each piece of dough to a circle 5 inches (13 cm) wide on a lightly floured surface. Lightly oil a frying pan and fry each tortilla over medium heat until it starts to brown, 30 seconds per side. Keep them warm until you are ready to serve. You may have a few extra tortillas.

When fish is ready, lay out the tortillas and place nasturtium leaves and flowers, avocado, tomatoes and onions down the center of each one. Top with a portion of fish and garnish with the cilantro and grated cheese. Drizzle the dressing overtop and serve with a wedge of lime on the side.

TIPS: Add just a little hot sauce at a time, tasting as you go, to get it perfectly spicy.

Turn store-bought soft tortillas into hard-shell tortillas by placing 1 tsp (5 mL) olive oil in a pan over medium heat. Fry the tortillas on each side for 15 seconds and then drape over a rolling pin to cool.

FOR THE TACOS

1 tsp (5 ml) saffron threads

½ tsp (2 ml) ground cumin

½ tsp (2 ml) cayenne pepper

1 tsp (5 ml) coarse kosher salt

¼ tsp (1 ml) freshly ground
   black pepper

1½ lb (675 g) white fish fillets
   (snapper or mahi mahi
   work well)

1 Tbsp (15 ml) salted butter

10–12 (8-inch/20 cm) tortillas
   (homemade, see above, or
   store-bought)

1 cup (250 ml) shredded
   nasturtium leaves and flowers,
   washed and dried
   (see page 128)

2 avocados, sliced

2 tomatoes, diced

½ red onion, diced

½ bunch cilantro leaves

1 cup (250 ml) grated pepper
   Jack cheese

1 lime, cut into wedges, to serve

Hot sauce makes everything better! The best hot sauces are fermented, which allows their flavors to develop and creates healthy bacteria. If you aren't well versed in fermentation, you may be a little intimidated by the process, but don't be. Fermenting is a wonderful skill to add to your culinary repertoire.

Nasturtium Hot Sauce

Prepare a 4-cup (1 L) mason jar for canning by boiling in a canning pot for 10 minutes. Using long tongs or a jar lifter, transfer the jar to a wire rack and allow to cool.

Pour the warm, filtered water into a large bowl and mix in the salt to create a brine.

Place the nasturtium flowers, chilies, garlic and honey in the mason jar. Pour in the brine. Weigh the veggies down so they don't stick up out of the water—this helps prevent them from going moldy. You can use a weight specially designed for this purpose or you can fill a sealable plastic bag with water and place it on top of the veggies to ensure they stay submerged.

Cover the jar with a fermentation lid (which lets out excess gas) or a couple of layers of cheesecloth. Place the jar on a plate to catch any overflow liquid, and set it aside in a cool, dark place. Let it ferment until the brine looks cloudy, 5–7 days.

Drain off the brine, reserving ½ cup (125 ml). Transfer the reserved brine to a blender. Add the vinegar. Blend until smooth.

Bottle and store in the fridge for up to 6 months.

TIPS: Use white or apple cider vinegar instead of sherry vinegar for a less sweet sauce.

Roasting your chilies on the barbecue until they are slightly burned will give your hot sauce a lovely smoky flavor.

MAKES ABOUT 1 CUP (250 ML)

Photo on page 138

3 cups (750 ml) warm filtered water (see tip)

1 Tbsp (15 ml) sea salt

1½ cups (375 ml) nasturtium flowers, washed and dried (see page 128)

24 small red Thai chilies, halved and deseeded (see tip)

5 cloves garlic, crushed

1 Tbsp (15 ml) honey

½ cup (125 ml) sherry vinegar (see tip)

TIPS: Tap water contains chlorine which inhibits the fermenting process, so use filtered water. Water should be heated to 110°F (45°C).

These chilies make for a fairly hot sauce; leave the seeds in for a hotter sauce. Use jalapeños for a milder sauce or a mixture of chilies for more flavor.

Wear gloves when you're cutting the chilies.

These salty little green delicacies are a particular favorite of mine. I love biting into a caper and getting that briny shot of flavor. Of course, you can eat them on all things salmon, but they're also delicious in oysters, or added to pasta dishes, salads, sandwiches, salsa, deviled eggs and dips. Nasturtium seeds make fantastic capers. Just make sure to gather them while they are green.

Nasturtium Capers

Prepare your jar for canning by boiling it in a pot of water for 10 minutes. Using long tongs or a jar lifter, transfer the jar to a wire rack and allow it to cool.

Drop the seeds into the jar and add the dill.

Place the vinegar, water, salt and sugar in a small pot and bring to a boil over high heat. When boiling, add sugar and salt and stir until dissolved. Pour the hot liquid over the seeds. Seal the jar and store in cool, dark place. Leave the seeds to pickle for a couple of weeks before you enjoy them.

Store the capers in the jar at room temperature for up to 6 months and for up to 3 weeks in the fridge after opening.

MAKES 2 CUPS (500 ML)

Photo on page 138

1 cup (250 ml) green nasturtium seeds (see page 129)

2 sprigs fresh dill (you can use thyme or a bay leaf if you're not into dill)

⅓ cup (75 ml) apple cider vinegar (organic if you can!)

⅓ cup (75 ml) water

1 Tbsp (15 ml) kosher or sea salt

½ tsp (2 ml) granulated sugar

These mini sweet pies are the perfect breakfast pie (although, what pie isn't?) and make great party treats or lunchbox surprises. If you have leftover pie pastry from another recipe, these tasty bad boys are the perfect way to avoid food waste.

. . . .

Party Time Hand Pies

To make the hand pies, sift the flour, salt and sugar into a large mixing bowl. Using your fingertips, rub in the butter until the mixture resembles bread crumbs. Add a tablespoon (15 ml) of ice water at a time to bring the dough together, being careful not to overwork it. Turn out the dough, shape it into a disk, cover it with plastic wrap and refrigerate for at least 30 minutes.

Preheat the oven to 350°F (175°C). Grease a baking sheet.

On a lightly floured surface, roll out the dough to ⅛-inch (0.25 cm) thick. Cut out 18 squares, each measuring 3.5 × 3.5 inches (9 × 9 cm). Spoon about 1 Tbsp (15 ml) nasturtium jelly into the center of a square, leaving ½-inch (1.3 cm) around the edge and cover with the other square. Using a fork, crimp the edges together and place on the baking sheet. Using a fork again, prick a few holes in the top of each pastry and gently brush the egg on using a pastry brush.

Bake until golden brown, 25–28 minutes. Place the baking sheet on a wire rack and leave the pastries to cool completely before glazing.

To make the glaze, sift the icing sugar into a medium bowl and add just enough milk to form a thick glaze that you can still spread easily. Glaze the top of each tart and add sprinkles.

Store the hand pies in a sealed container in the fridge for up to 3 days.

MAKES 9 HAND PIES

FOR THE HAND PIES

2½ cups (625 ml) all-purpose flour

¼ tsp (1 ml) table salt

1 Tbsp (15 ml) granulated sugar

1 cup (250 ml) cold salted butter, cut into cubes

½ cup (125 ml) ice-cold water

½ cup plus 2 tsp (135 mL) Nasturtium Jelly (page 146; see tip)

1 medium egg, lightly beaten

FOR THE GLAZE

¾ cup (175 ml) icing sugar

1 Tbsp (15 ml) 2% milk

Sprinkles, for decorating

TIPS: Of course, you can use another jam or jelly as a filling! Or pop a couple of fresh berries and a little sugar in the center if you prefer a more traditional pie.

HIBISCUS
JELLY
(page 185)

PEONY JAM
(page 58)

DANDELION JAM
(page 16)

VIOLET JELLY
(page 49)

TRADITIONAL
CREAM SCONES
WITH
NASTURTIUM
JELLY
(page 147)

The peppery flavor of the nasturtium flowers gives this jelly a delightfully unexpected kick. Jellies are jams without the fruit or flowers in them. We generally remove the flowers to prevent a bitter taste, but some, like dandelion and rose jams, can stay in. This jelly works on toast, scones and bagels, but is equally yummy on a charcuterie board with some crackers and a really good cheese.

Nasturtium Jelly

Prepare your jars for canning by boiling them in a canning pot of water for 10 minutes. Using long tongs or a jar lifter, transfer the jars to a wire rack and allow to cool.

Place the nasturtium flowers in a medium pot, add the apple juice and bring just to a boil over medium heat. Turn the heat off and leave to cool on the burner. Ideally, you should cover the pot and leave the nasturtium flowers to steep overnight for deeper flavor and color, but if you're in a rush, you can steep them for an hour.

Strain out the flowers, but don't squeeze them or your jelly will have a bitter aftertaste. Discard the flowers.

Pour the apple juice into a large pot. Add the sugar and lemon juice, mix to combine and bring to a boil over medium heat, stirring occasionally. Mix in the pectin and let the mixture boil hard for 1 minute. Remove the pot from the heat. The color of the jelly will depend on the colors of the flowers you used. If you want to augment the color, add a couple of drops of food coloring now.

Spoon the jelly into the jars and seal the lids firmly. Check the water level in your canning pot, place the jars back into the pot and boil them for 10 minutes. Using long tongs or a jar lifter, transfer the jars to a wire rack to cool.

Store this jelly in the jars at room temperature for 1 year and for 1 month in the fridge after opening.

MAKES 4–5 CUPS
(1–1.25 L)
Photo on page 48

1 cup (250 ml) nasturtium
  flowers, washed and dried
  (see page 128)
3 cups (750 ml) unsweetened
  apple juice
4 cups (1 L) granulated sugar
¼ cup (60 ml) freshly squeezed
  lemon juice (1–2 lemons)
1 (1¾ oz/49 g) package
  powdered pectin (see tip)
Food coloring (optional)

TIPS: Use diabetic pectin if you want to omit the sugar. Diabetic pectin will set without sugar. You can either leave sugar out completely or substitute a natural sweetener instead. This pectin will ensure the jelly sets properly.

There are as many ways to make a scone as the day is long. For me, the best way to make scones is to cut them small and round so you can eat half a scone in two bites. They should puff up so you can break them in two with ease. And they should be crispy on the outside and soft on the inside—the perfect vehicle for a teaspoon of jelly and a dollop of cream. Eat them on Sundays with someone you love, preferably in your PJs.

Traditional Cream Scones with Nasturtium Jelly

Preheat the oven to 350°F (175°C). Grease a baking sheet.

Sift the flour, baking powder, sugar and salt into a large bowl. Using your fingertips, rub in the butter until the mixture resembles bread crumbs. Add just enough milk to bring the ingredients together and, using a fork, mix to form a soft dough, being careful not to overwork it.

On a lightly floured surface, roll out the dough to about 1 inch (2.5 cm) thick. Using a 2-inch (5 cm) round cookie cutter, cut out scones and place them on the baking sheet. Gather and re-roll dough, if needed. Brush the top of each scone with egg.

Bake until golden brown, 12–15 minutes. Place the baking sheet on a wire rack and leave the scones to cool completely.

Gently slice the cooled scones in half horizontally and spread about 1½ tsp (7 ml) of jam over each half.

To whip the cream, place the chilled cream and icing sugar in the bowl of your stand mixer fitted with the whisk attachment. Whisk on high speed until medium peaks form, when the cream can just hold its shape. Top your jam scones with whipped cream and, if you have them, garnish with a nasturtium flower.

Store the scones in an airtight container at room temperature for 2–3 days.

MAKES 9 SCONES

Photo on page 145

2 cups (500 ml) all-purpose flour

4 tsp (20 ml) baking powder

4 tsp (20 ml) icing sugar

¼ tsp (1 ml) table salt

¼ cup (60 ml) cold salted butter, cut into cubes

½ cup (125 ml) whole milk (see tip)

1 large egg, lightly beaten

½ cup (125 ml) Nasturtium Jelly (page 146)

1½ cups (375 ml) whipping cream, chilled

2 Tbsp icing sugar

Nasturtium flowers, washed and dried (see page 129), for garnish (optional)

TIP: Sour cream or buttermilk work really well instead of the milk in this recipe. Use the same quantities, but expect a richer flavor.

12. GENUS: *ROSA*

PERENNIAL

. . . .

IDENTIFICATION:

Roses fall into three broad categories: bush, shrub and climbing. They all have thorny stems (canes) and dark green, heart-shaped leaves with serrated edges. Their flowers can be a single whirl of petals around the stamen or several layers, depending on the variety.

GROWING:

Most roses flower in the spring, some flower all summer long and others offer a spring and fall flush. Roses like full sun and should get 6–8 hours of sunlight daily. They like rich, well-drained loamy soil and should be planted in early spring when the danger of frost has passed. Wait until the temperature of the soil is 40°F–60°F (4.5°C–15.5°C).

Fertilize your roses throughout the growing season. Prune them in the fall or winter, sanitizing your pruners as you move between plants to prevent the spread of disease.

Water your roses every two to three days, and more frequently when the heat of summer hits. Blooming roses will need a little extra water, so pay attention to the flowers—if they start to droop, it's time for a drink (the roses, not you!).

When drying roses, shake out the blooms to free any bugs. Carefully pick the petals and discard the stems. Rinse petals and pat dry with a paper towel. Lay petals on a paper towel in a dry place for 3–4 days.

Rose

Fossil records show that roses have been around for 35 million years, which means there are more varieties than you can count in a month of Sundays. The Greeks believed Aphrodite created roses from her tears, while Cleopatra is said to have doused the sails of her ship in rosewater, emitting the scent of roses as she floated down the Nile. It's only natural that roses have become the symbol of romantic love, and I wouldn't have it any other way.

Harissa is a spicy, earthy North African paste that's really good to have in your fridge to add instant flavor to all your favorite dishes. Use it as a rub on meats, or in tacos, tagines, curries or poke bowls. It also makes a wonderful gift for friends and family.

. . . .

Rose Harissa Spice

Rehydrate the dried chilies in a little water then finely chop.

Place 1 Tbsp (15 ml) of the oil in a small frying pan and warm it over medium heat. Add the coriander, cumin and caraway seeds and fry until fragrant, about 20 seconds.

Remove the pan from the heat. Using a slotted spoon, scoop out the seeds, leaving the oil in the pan. Place the seeds in a mortar and pestle, add the rose petals and paprika, and grind into a paste.

Add 1 Tbsp (15 ml) of oil to the pan, place over medium heat and add the serrano chilies, shallots and garlic. Fry until soft, about 3 minutes.

Place the spice paste, fried chili mix, rose water, tomato paste, lemon juice, sugar, salt, apple cider vinegar and remaining oil in a blender and blend to a smooth paste.

Store the harissa in an airtight container in the fridge for 11 months.

MAKES 10 SERVINGS

10 dried smoked chili peppers
½ cup (125 ml) extra virgin olive oil, divided
1½ tsp (7 ml) coriander seeds
1 tsp (5 ml) cumin seeds
1 tsp (5 ml) caraway seeds
1 Tbsp (15 ml) dried rose petals (see page 148)
2 tsp (10 ml) smoked paprika
2 serrano chilies, chopped and deseeded
1 Tbsp (15 ml) finely chopped shallot
4 cloves garlic, finely chopped
2 Tbsp (30 ml) Rose Water (page 165 or store-bought)
1 Tbsp (15 ml) tomato paste
2 Tbsp (30 ml) freshly squeezed lemon juice
1½ tsp (7 ml) granulated sugar
½ tsp (2 ml) coarse kosher salt
¼ cup (60 ml) apple cider vinegar

If you prefer a dry rub, try this tasty alternative.

. . . .

Rose Harissa
Dry Rub

Using a blender or using mortar and pestle, grind all the
ingredients together.

Store the rub in an airtight container in a cool, dry place
for up to 1 year.

MAKES 10 SERVINGS

10 dried, smoked chili peppers

2 Tbsp (30 ml) cumin seeds

2 Tbsp (30 ml) coriander seeds

1½ Tbsp (22 ml) caraway seeds

2 Tbsp (30 ml) smoked paprika

1½ tsp (7 ml) garlic powder

1 tsp (5 ml) coarse kosher salt

1 tsp (5 ml) dried parsley

1 tsp (5 ml) dried oregano

1 Tbsp (15 ml) dried rose petals
 (see page 148)

I love butternut squash, mostly because it's much easier to peel and chop than other squash. It has the added bonus of being bright and delicious. You can eat the flowers, and the seeds are sensational when roasted.

· ·

Summer Squash Salad

Preheat the oven to 350°F (175°C).

Cut the squash in half and use a spoon to remove the seeds. Place the seeds in a colander and rinse until they aren't slippery anymore and all the squash string has been removed. Set aside to dry.

Peel the squash and cut it into 2-inch (5 cm) chunks. Place the chunks in a medium bowl, add the harissa paste and toss with enough oil to coat everything evenly.

Roast on a greased baking sheet until the squash is soft and cooked through, about 50 minutes.

Place the seeds on a baking sheet and coat with about 1 Tbsp (15 ml) olive oil and the salt. Roast alongside the squash until they begin to brown, about 15 minutes. Give the baking sheet a shake halfway through roasting to turn the seeds.

Let the squash and the seeds cool on the pan.

Place the squash, avocado, greens and mozzarella in a salad bowl and drizzle with the vinegar. Top with the seeds for a crunchy finish.

SERVES 6

Photo on page 84

1 medium butternut squash
Extra virgin olive oil
2 Tbsp (30 ml) Rose Harissa
  Spice (page 150)
½ tsp (2 ml) coarse kosher salt
2 avocados, sliced
4 cups (1 L) salad greens
Half 6 oz (170 g) ball mozzarella,
  shredded
1 Tbsp (15 ml) sherry vinegar

In our little farming village, two things are sacred: pie and jam. Our local jam-makers have a few essential ingredients: recipes passed down through generations, homegrown fruit and heaps of heart and soul. We know our jam, and we all agree that this rose jam is sensational! It's delicate, delicious and fragrant. It's as perfect on scones, muffins and toast as it is on a charcuterie board.

. . . .

Rose Jam

Prepare your jars and lids for canning by boiling them in a canning pot for 10 minutes. Using long tongs or a jar lifter, transfer the jars to a wire rack and allow to cool.

Put the boiling water in a large heatproof bowl, add the rose petals and leave to steep for 2 hours to make rose tea.

Strain out the petals but don't squeeze them, as this will give the jam a bitter aftertaste. Set the petals aside.

Pour the rose water into a pot, mix in the lemon juice and pectin and set it over high heat. Bring it to a rolling boil that can't be stirred down.

Add the sugar all at once and return to a boil, stirring constantly. Boil for 1 minute and then remove from the heat. Skim off any foam from the top of the jam.

Scoop the jam into the jars and seal lids tightly. Check the water level in your canning pot, place the jars back in the pot and boil them for 10 minutes.

Store jam at room temperature for up to 1 year, and once opened, in the fridge for 1 month.

MAKES 5–6 CUPS (1.25–1.5 L)

4 cups (1 L) boiling water

1 cup (250 ml) dried or
2 cups (500 ml) fresh rose petals, rinsed and dried (see page 148)

1 tsp (5 ml) freshly squeezed lemon juice

1 (1¾ oz/49 g) package powdered pectin

4 cups (1 L) granulated sugar

For me, Sunday afternoons have always been for baking. This was one of the very first recipes I learned to bake as a child, and it still makes me think happy thoughts of jammy fingers and afternoon tea.

. . . .

Tea Squares

Preheat the oven to 350°F (175°C). Grease a 9-inch (23 cm) square baking pan.

Sift the flour and baking powder into a medium bowl.

In the bowl of your stand mixer, or in a separate bowl using a hand mixer, cream the butter, oil, sugar and egg on medium speed until light in color, about 2 minutes. Add the dry ingredients to the butter mixture and mix on low speed until a soft dough forms. Divide the dough in 2 evenly sized pieces. Wrap one half in plastic wrap and refrigerate for 10 minutes.

Press the other half of the dough into the bottom of the prepared pan. Spread the rose jam evenly over the dough, getting right to the edges, and then grate the remaining dough over the top.

Bake until the dough begins to brown on the top, 15–20 minutes. Remove the pan from the oven and, using a sharp knife, cut the hot dough into squares while it's still in the pan. Leave to cool completely in the pan and then gently remove them from the pan.

Store the tea squares in an airtight container at room temperature for 3–4 days.

MAKES 24 SQUARES

Photo on page 157

1¼ cups (300 ml) all-purpose
   flour
1½ tsp (7 ml) baking powder
¼ cup (60 ml) salted butter,
   at room temperature
1 Tbsp (15 ml) vegetable oil
3 Tbsp (45 ml) granulated sugar
1 medium egg
1 cup (250 ml) Rose Jam
   (page 153)

Pavlova is a lovely light meringue base topped with fresh fruit and cream—a classic light dessert that's perfect for hot summer nights. New Zealand claims the pavlova was the brainchild of a Wellington hotel chef who took inspiration from ballerina Anna Pavlova's tutu. Australians dispute this, saying that it was created in a hotel in Perth— also inspired by Anna and her tutu.

The world's largest pavlova, Pavzilla, was first baked in February 1999 in Wellington, New Zealand, and measured 147 feet (just under 45 meters) in diameter. Not to be outdone, students from the Eastern Institute of Technology in Auckland, New Zealand, created Pavkong in March 2005. It measured 210 feet (64 meters).

Rose Pavlova

Before you begin, wash the bowl and whisk attachment of your stand mixer in warm soapy water and rinse thoroughly. If there is any grease on your equipment, your meringue won't stiffen.

Preheat the oven to 275°F (135°C). Line a baking sheet with parchment paper and trace a 7-inch (18 cm) circle in the center.

To make the pavlova, using a stand mixer fitted with the whisk attachment, whip the egg whites on high speed until frothy. With the mixer running, slowly add the sugar, 1 Tbsp (15 ml) at a time, until stiff, glossy peaks form. Turn off the mixer and sprinkle the cornstarch, rose water and vinegar over the eggs. Using a spatula gently fold them into the egg whites.

Scoop the meringue out onto the circle and spread it evenly around, leaving a small well in the center for the filling.

Bake until the meringue turns an eggshell pink, about 1 hour and 15 minutes.

continues

SERVES 8

FOR THE PAVLOVA

4 large egg whites, at
   room temperature

1 cup (250 ml) superfine sugar

1½ tsp (7 ml) cornstarch

1 Tbsp (15 ml) Rose Water
   (page 165 or store-bought)

1 tsp (5 ml) white vinegar

Turn the oven off and prop open the door a little while you prepare the filling. Let cool for at least 20 minutes to avoid cracking.

To make the filling, using a stand mixer fitted with the whisk attachment, whip the cream, rose water and icing sugar on high speed until smooth and combined, about 2 minutes. Dollop the filling into the well in the pavlova and top with seasonal berries and nuts. Sprinkle with icing sugar and serve immediately.

FOR THE FILLING

½ cup (125 ml) whipping (35%) cream

1 tsp (5 ml) Rose Water (page 165 or store-bought)

½ cup (125 ml) icing sugar, plus extra for sprinkling

Seasonal berries and ⅓ cup (80 ml) pecan pieces (see tip)

TIP: You can use any fruit and nut combination for the topping.

ROSE PAVLOVA
(page 155)

TEA SQUARES
(page 154)

ROSE SIMPLE
SYRUP
(page 164)

THE ROSALINE
(page 164)

ROSE TURKISH
DELIGHT
(page 159)

If you're intimidated by the thought of making your own candy, let me tell you that it's easier than you think. Sure, it requires attentiveness, precision and boatloads of patience, but if five-year-old you could see you now, they would be so proud to know that you grew up to be the kind of person who makes their own damn candy.

. . . .

Rose Turkish Delight

Line a 9-inch (23 cm) square baking pan with parchment paper and spray it with nonstick cooking spray.

Place the sugar, 1½ cups (375 ml) of the water and the lemon juice in a medium pot and place over medium heat. Stir until the sugar is dissolved, then bring the mixture to a gentle boil, still over medium heat. Brush the sides of your pot with a wet basting brush to prevent sugar crystals forming.

Place a candy thermometer in the pot to measure the temperature. Keep heating the mixture, stirring from time to time, until it reaches 240°F (115.5°C), about 45 minutes.

When the sugar mixture is at about 220°F (104°C), start the next part of the recipe.

Place 2½ cups (625 ml) of water in a large pot over medium heat. Use the remaining ½ cup (125 ml) water to make a paste with the cornstarch, cream of tartar and salt in a small bowl. Slowly add the paste to the water in the pot, stirring until it is smooth and lump-free. Bring the cornstarch mixture to a boil over medium heat, stirring constantly, until it thickens.

continues

MAKES 25 SQUARES

4 cups (1 L) granulated sugar

4½ cups (1.125 L) water, divided

1 Tbsp (15 ml) freshly squeezed lemon juice

1¼ cups (300 ml) cornstarch

1 tsp (5 ml) cream of tartar

½ tsp (2 ml) fine kosher salt

1½ Tbsp (22 ml) Rose Water (page 165 or store-bought)

Red food coloring, optional

1½ cups (375 ml) icing sugar

Once the sugar mixture is at 240°F (115.5°C), gently whisk it into the cornstarch mixture. Turn down the heat to low, and simmer until the mixture is golden yellow and very thick, 8–10 minutes, stirring frequently.

Remove the pot from the heat and mix in the rose water and food coloring. Add just a drop or two of food coloring at a time until you achieve the color you want. Pour the mixture gently into the prepared pan and leave, uncovered, overnight to set.

Dust a work surface with icing sugar and turn out the Turkish delight. Peel off the parchment paper and dust the bottom with icing sugar as well. Use an oiled knife to cut the candy into 1.8-inch (4.5 cm) squares. Coat each square with icing sugar.

High-five your five-year-old self and have candy for breakfast!

Store the Turkish delight in an airtight container at room temperature for 3–5 days.

Food should be everyone's love language. It engages all five senses and, when made with love, will evoke that same feeling in those you feed. Food memories can take you right back to a good time or great person. This recipe always evokes one of my favorites. When I was doing some travel writing, I once found myself in a souk in the Middle East. I had been struggling with the area's strong, bitter coffee, which was a far cry from my usual foamy lattes. As I sat feeling sorry for myself, a kindly waiter brought me a slice of a Persian love cake. The stickiness on my fingers, the subtle smell of rose and the moist sweetness were the perfect antidote to the bitter black coffee.

Persian Love Cake

Preheat the oven to 320°F (160°C). Grease two 9-inch (23 cm) round cake pans.

To make the cake, using a stand mixer fitted with the paddle attachment, cream the butter and sugar on medium speed, until light and fluffy, about 5 minutes. Add the eggs one at a time, beating well after each addition. In a separate bowl, sift in the flour, baking powder, cardamom and salt. Add dry ingredients to the butter mixture ½ cup (125 ml) at a time, alternating with lemon zest and juice and rosewater. Mix well to combine. Scrape down the sides and bottom of the bowl as needed. Once the batter is combined, divide it evenly between the cake pans.

Bake until a skewer inserted into the center of each comes out clean, about 45 minutes. Place the cake pans on wire racks while you make the syrup.

To make the syrup, place the sugar, water and lemon juice in a small pot and bring to a boil over medium heat, stirring occasionally. Turn down the heat to low and simmer until all the sugar has melted, 3–5 minutes. Using a skewer, prick holes into the still-hot cakes and pour the syrup overtop.

continues

MAKES ONE DOUBLE-LAYER
9-INCH (23 CM) CAKE

FOR THE CAKE

7 oz (200 g) unsalted butter

¾ cup (175 ml) granulated sugar

4 medium eggs

1¾ cups (425 ml) all-purpose
  flour

2 tsp (10 ml) baking powder

1 tsp (5 ml) ground cardamom

Pinch table salt

Zest of ½ lemon

2 Tbsp (30 ml) freshly squeezed
  lemon juice

2 Tbsp (30 ml) Rose Water
  (page 165 or store-bought)

½ cup (125 ml) Rose Jam
  (page 153, or another jam
  if you prefer)

Let the cakes cool completely in the pans. Place one cake on a cake stand and spread the jam evenly on it. Place the second cake on top and sandwich them together.

To make the icing, place the sugar and lemon juice in a small bowl. Mix in just enough water to make a thick icing. Pour over the cake, using a spatula to spread it evenly, and top with pistachios and rose petals.

Keep the cake in an airtight container in the fridge for up to 3 days.

FOR THE SYRUP

2 Tbsp (30 ml) granulated sugar

¼ cup (60 ml) water

1 Tbsp (15 ml) freshly squeezed lemon juice

FOR THE ICING

¾ cup (175 ml) icing sugar

1 Tbsp (15 ml) freshly squeezed lemon juice

2 Tbsp (30 ml) cold water

⅓ cup (75 ml) chopped pistachios

2 Tbsp (30 ml) rose petals, washed and dried (see page 148)

PERSIAN
LOVE CAKE
(page 161)

The delicate floral fragrance and flavour of rose syrup adds a touch of romance to any drink.

. . . .

Rose Simple Syrup

Put the boiling water in a large heatproof bowl, add the rose petals and leave to steep for 2 hours to make rose tea. Strain out the petals, but don't squeeze them or the syrup will have a bitter aftertaste. Discard the petals. Place the rose tea and sugar in a small pot and bring to a boil over high heat. Stir until the sugar dissolves, then remove from the heat and leave to cool.

Store the syrup in an airtight container in the fridge for 1 month.

TIP: Add a splash of rose syrup to regular water, tonic, club soda or sparkling water and ice on a summer day for a divine fragrant alternative to soda pop.

MAKES 1 CUP (250 ML)
Photo on page 104

1 cup (250 ml) boiling water
1 cup (250 ml) dried rose petals
  (see page 148) or 2 cups
  (500 ml) fresh petals, washed
  and dried (see page 148)
1 cup (250 ml) granulated sugar

TIP: The rose simple syrup can be added to cocktails, poured over pancakes or enjoyed over ice cream.

Have your rose and drink it too! This sweet drink, the Rosaline will ensure you enjoy the hell out of your roses.

. . . .

The Rosaline

Fill a tall glass halfway with ice. Add the wine, water, lemon juice and rose syrup. Give it all a good stir and garnish with a fresh rose petal.

SERVES 1
Photo on page 158

Ice cubes
4 oz (125 ml) sparkling rosé wine
2 Tbsp (30 ml) sparkling water
1 Tbsp (15 ml) freshly squeezed
  lemon juice
1 Tbsp (15 ml) Rose Syrup
  (see above)
1 fresh rose petal, washed
  and dried (see page 148),
  for garnish

Rose water is romantically fragrant and luxuriously lavish, which is why it's one of my favorite things. I love to give bottles of it as a gift in the summer. If you're using it to cook, I suggest you use the distillation method, as the taste will be far more pronounced.

. . . .

Rose Water

To make the rose water on the stovetop, place the water and petals in a medium pot and bring to a boil over high heat. Boil for 10 minutes. Remove from the heat, cover and leave to cool. Strain out the petals, but don't squeeze them or the rose water may have a bitter aftertaste. Store in a sealable container and use within 1 week or keep in the fridge for up to 3 months.

To use the distillation method, place a heatproof jug in the center of a large pot. The jug must be shorter than the pot. Place the petals in the pot and fill it so the water comes about halfway up the side of the jug. Place the lid on the pot upside down so the lowest part (i.e., the pot lid handle) is over the jug. Bring the water to a very gentle simmer over medium heat.

Place some ice cubes in a sealable plastic bag and place the bag on the upturned pot lid when the water begins to simmer. This will help to cool the water vapor which will condense and drip down into the jug. Replace the ice cubes as they melt. Continue to simmer the water until you have collected about 1 cup (250 ml) rose water in the jug.

Pour the rose water from the jug into a mason jar. It will last up to 1 month on the counter or up to 6 months in the fridge.

MAKES ABOUT 1 CUP (250 ML)

FOR THE STOVETOP METHOD

1½ cups (375 ml) water

¼ cup (60 ml) dried rose petals or ¾ cup (175 ml) fresh petals, washed and dried (see page 148)

FOR THE DISTILLATION METHOD

1½ cups (375 ml) dried rose petals or 5 cups (1.25 L) fresh petals, washed and dried (see page 148)

Water

Ice cubes

13. GENUS: *CUCURBITA PEPO*   **ANNUAL**

. . . .

IDENTIFICATION:

Zucchini squash range in color from dark green to bright yellow. The elongated fruits can have stripes or a solid color. The round green leaves grow to 12 inches (30 cm) in diameter or wider. The leaf stalks are thick and hollow and covered in prickly hairs. Squash plants are an annual crop, so they need to be resown each spring.

Squash plants produce both male and female flowers on the same plant. There will be many more males than females. The males will not produce fruit, so they can be picked without compromising your squash harvest. They have no pistils and their stalks are long and slender. Female flowers grow closer to the center of the plant and have a bulbous embryonic fruit where the flower meets the stem.

GROWING:

Sow the seeds directly into the soil as soon as the last chance of frost has passed. Zucchini squash love warmth, so create little mounds of soil to plant them in. This practice is known as "hilling." It lets the sun warm the soil more effectively and will provide good drainage. Plant zucchini squash plants together to encourage pollination. The plant will produce mostly male flowers at first, which you can pick for the recipes in this book. When the female flowers appear, you can still pick the males. Just brush the pollen off onto the female flowers to ensure pollination and fruiting. Fruit should appear 50–60 days after planting.

Water the zucchini with 1 inch (2.5 cm) of water each week and use mulch to retain the moisture and protect the plants from any cold weather or unexpected late frost.

Beware the squash vine borers, which lay their eggs in the stems. You can avoid an invasion of these creatures by waiting until July to plant as the borer moths will already have laid their eggs elsewhere.

After picking the flowers, shake out any bugs, then rinse and pat dry with a paper towel. Store flowers in a sealable plastic bag in the fridge for up to 3 days.

Zucchini Squash Flowers

My first foray into vegetable gardening left me with an infestation of zucchini. I thought six plants sounded reasonable for a family of two, but I was so, so wrong. Zucchini plants produce at such a rapid rate that even the most gregarious vegetarians would struggle to work through the fruits of one plant.

Apparently, I'm not the only one who made this mistake, as the neighbors would pretend to be out when I came bearing gifts of zucchini squash (again!). Instead, I started harvesting the flowers, which are just gorgeous to eat. Then six became the perfect number of zucchini plants to have after all.

For the recipes in this book, you can substitute the flowers of any winter squash varieties for the zucchini flowers. Squash blossoms are silky and mild and taste a little like the squash themselves.

SQUASH
FLOWER PIZZA
(page 170)

ZUCCINI FLOWER AND
ACORN SQUASH SOUP
(page 169)

This is a great fall recipe! It's a super way to use all your extra zucchini flowers and enjoy the first acorn squash of the season at the same time. The color is such a beautiful yellow—it's like sunshine in a bowl!

. . . .

Zucchini Flower and Acorn Squash Soup

Preheat the oven to 375°F (190°C).

Halve and peel the squashes. Using a spoon, scoop out and discard the seeds. Chop the squash into 1-inch (2.5 cm) cubes and place in a medium bowl. Use 3 Tbsp (45 ml) of the oil to coat the squash and place the squash in a roasting pan.

Roast until tender, 30–40 minutes.

Place the remaining 3 Tbsp (45 ml) of oil in a large soup pot and warm it over low heat. Add the onion, cover and fry until soft, about 3 minutes. Add the garlic, ginger, zucchini flowers and sage, mix together and cook over low heat until fragrant, about 2 minutes. Add 1 Tbsp (15 ml) oil if it begins to stick.

Mix in the broth, turn up the heat to medium and cook for 15 minutes, stirring occasionally.

Transfer the acorn squash and broth mixture to a blender or food processor fitted with the steel blade and blend until smooth. Taste the soup before you add any salt. Depending on the kind of broth you use, the soup might be salty enough. Add pepper, to taste.

Stir in the cream and serve hot with a crusty bread.

Store the soup in an airtight container in the fridge for 3 days.

SERVES 4

2 large acorn squashes

6 Tbsp (90 ml) extra virgin olive oil, divided

1 large red onion, chopped

3 cloves garlic, finely chopped

2-inch (5 cm) piece of fresh ginger, peeled and finely chopped

24 zucchini flowers, washed and dried (see page 166)

3 Tbsp (45 ml) chopped fresh sage leaves

5 cups (1.25 L) chicken or vegetable broth

Kosher salt and freshly ground black pepper, to taste

½ cup (125 ml) whipping (35%) cream

I love eating this pizza outside in the late summer sunshine. It's great with a cold beer or a nice white wine. The delicately flavored toppings shine through, thanks to the lack of tomato sauce and strong meats like salami. Definitely feel free to experiment with toppings you think may work well here, but try to keep them balanced!

Squash Flower Pizza

To make the dough, place the water in a small bowl and sprinkle in the yeast and sugar. Set aside until frothy, 5–10 minutes.

Sift the flour and salt in a large bowl and mix to combine. Add the yeast mixture and mix until a sticky dough forms. Flour your hands and then knead the dough until soft and malleable, about 10 minutes. If you prefer, you can use a stand mixer fitted with the dough hook to mix the dough on medium speed for about 2 minutes.

Oil a large mixing bowl and place the dough inside. Cover with plastic wrap or a damp tea towel and leave in a warm spot until doubled in size, 2–3 hours.

Punch down the dough and keep covered with plastic wrap or a damp tea towel at room temperature until needed, about half an hour.

Preheat the oven to 500°F (260°C). Oil a large (14 inch/35 cm) pizza pan.

On a lightly floured surface, roll out the dough to a 14-inch (35 cm) circle. Place the dough on the prepared pan and brush the top with ¼ cup (60 ml) of the oil, getting right to the edges of the dough. Top the pizza with the cheeses, leaving a thin edge.

Bake until the crust begins to brown, about 8 minutes.

MAKES ONE 14-INCH (35 CM) PIZZA
Photo on page 168

FOR THE DOUGH

¾ cup (175 ml) water, heated to 110°F (45°C)

1 envelope (2¼ tsp/11 ml) active dry yeast

1½ tsp (7 ml) granulated sugar

2 cups (500 ml) all-purpose flour, plus extra for dusting

1 tsp (5 ml) coarse kosher salt

FOR THE TOPPING

⅓ cup (75 ml) extra virgin olive oil, divided

1 cup (250 ml) grated mozzarella

½ cup (125 ml) fresh ricotta

¼ cup (60 ml) finely grated Parmesan

12 medium zucchini flowers, washed and dried (see page 166), base and stamens removed and petals cut into thin strips

1 cup (250 ml) fresh basil leaves

Drizzle the zucchini flowers with the remaining 1 Tbsp (15 ml) of oil and toss to coat. Remove the pizza from the oven, arrange the zucchini flowers over the top and bake until the flowers just begin to wilt, about 2 minutes. Remove the pizza from the oven and arrange fresh basil leaves over the top. Serve immediately.

Store leftovers in a sealed container in the fridge for up to 3 days.

TIP: Add chili flakes or fresh red chilies to taste if you like a little spice.

In the spring, I can't wait to eat dinners outside. On the first nice evening in June, I'll set up the dinner table under the big maple in our front yard and enjoy this pasta under the setting summer sun. This is a quick and easy summer pasta that's light, colorful and super tasty. The pistachio nuts add a wonderful crunchy element, while the lemon zest gives it a satisfying tang.

Squash Petal Pasta

Fill a large pot halfway with water and enough salt to make it as salty as the sea. Bring to a boil over high heat and cook the pasta according to the package directions.

Meanwhile, place the oil in a large skillet and warm it over medium heat. Add the garlic and fry for 1 minute. Mix in the zucchini and fry until just soft, about 2 minutes. Mix in the petals and pistachios and fry for another 2 minutes until the petals wilt.

Drain the cooked pasta.

Remove the skillet from the heat. Add the pasta, cream and lemon zest and gently stir to combine. Add salt and pepper to taste. Scatter the Parmesan cheese over the top and tear up the basil leaves to garnish. Serve hot.

Store leftovers in a container in the fridge for up to 3 days.

SERVES 4

4 cups (1 L) bowtie pasta
Kosher salt
2 Tbsp (30 ml) extra virgin
   olive oil
2 garlic cloves, peeled and
   lightly crushed
2 medium zucchinis, thinly
   sliced in strips (see tip)
4 zucchini flowers, petals
   only, washed and dried
   (see page 166)
¼ cup (60 ml) chopped roasted
   pistachio nuts
⅔ cup (150 ml) whipping (35%)
   cream
Zest of 1 lemon
Sea salt and freshly ground
   black pepper, to taste
Finely grated Parmesan,
   to serve
¼ cup (60 ml) fresh basil leaves

TIP: Use a vegetable peeler or mandolin to slice thin slices down the side of the zucchini to create elegant ribbons.

ROASTED VEGGIE SALAD
WITH SAFFRON (page 194)

SQUASH PETAL PASTA
(page 172)

ODE TO
CRISPY FRIED
CHICKEN
(page 198)

FRIED
ZUCCHINI
FOWERS
(page 175)

Blooming zucchinis! This recipe is a great way to cull your zucchini crop. Choose the male flowers—females have a tiny zucchini fruit just behind the petals—if you don't want to miss out on your zucchini squash. These make a fantastic appetizer or snack when you're watching the game. They're great on their own, or you can bulk them out with filling. A spicy mayonnaise makes a great dip too!

. . . .

Fried Zucchini Flowers

Place the flour, kosher salt and beer in a medium bowl and whisk to combine. It's okay if there are a couple of lumps—it's more important not to whisk the beer flat. Fold in the egg whites.

Place about 2 inches (5 cm) of oil in a medium pot and warm it over low heat. You'll know it's ready when a little batter floats and turns brown after 1 minute.

Line a plate with paper towels.

Dip the zucchini flowers in the batter and, working in batches, gently place them in the oil. Fry on both sides until light brown, 2–3 minutes in total. Use a slotted spoon to transfer the zucchini flowers to the prepared plate. Season to taste with the sea salt and serve immediately.

SERVES 6

1¼ cups (300 ml) all-purpose
   flour
1 tsp (5 ml) coarse kosher salt
1 (12 oz/340 mL) can lager beer
3 large egg whites, beaten to
   stiff peaks
Vegetable oil, for frying
24 zucchini flowers, washed
   and dried and stamens
   removed (see page 166)
Sea salt

14.

13. GENUS: *HIBISCUS ROSA-SINENSIS*   **PERENNIAL**

. . . .

IDENTIFICATION:

The hibiscus is a shrub with dark green, glossy leaves with serrated edges. It is densely foliated, and reaches a height of 7–12 feet (2–3.5 meters). The large flowers have five petals and a protruding stamen packed with pollen.

GROWING:

The tropical varieties of these plants will be annuals in colder climates, but if you grow them in containers, you can bring them indoors over the winter. There are hardy varieties that are able to overwinter in colder climates. Here's a general list of the varieties.

Chinese hibiscus: tropical (*Hibiscus rosa-sinensis*)
Confederate rose: hardy (*Hibiscus mutabilis*)
Rose mallow: hardy (*Hibiscus moschuetos*)
Rose of Sharon: hardy (*Hibiscus syriacus*)
Texas star: hardy (*Hibiscus moschetos*)

Grow your hibiscus in sandy, loam soil in full sun. The soil should be very well-drained and your hibiscus should be watered about twice a week. If you are growing it in a container, water it every second day. Use warm water for container plants to prevent shock.

Pick the flowers and shake them out to free any bugs. Rinse them and pat dry with a paper towel. Lay the flowers on a paper towel in a dry place for 3-5 days for dried flowers.

Hibiscus

The gorgeous, flamboyant hibiscus flower lasts for a single day and is a symbol of ephemeral beauty, romantic love and passion. I started growing them in containers to attract hummingbirds to the garden, as they love the red flowers, but hibiscus is delicious to eat too. Hibiscus has a deep, rich tartness that is reminiscent of cranberries and it's packed with vitamin C.

The recipes in this book use Chinese hibiscus (*Hibiscus rosa-sinensis*), which you can grow yourself or purchase dried at most health-food stores, where it is sold for use as a tea.

These tacos are so good, they refuse to be served only on Tuesdays. You can eat the hibiscus flower petals and they make a great substitute for meat or fish in your favorite taco recipes. Making Hibiscus Simple Syrup or jam? Team up with these tacos so you reduce your food waste and use the whole flower.

. . . .

Hibiscus Tacos

Put the boiling water in a large heatproof bowl, add the hibiscus flowers and leave to steep for 15 minutes to soften and to make hibiscus tea. Strain out the flowers, but don't squeeze them or the tea will be bitter. Set the flowers aside.

Place the oil in a large frying pan and warm it over medium heat. Add the onions and garlic and fry until soft, about 3 minutes. Stir in the chili powder, cumin, salt, oregano and paprika. If the spices cause the taco mix to stick, add 1 Tbsp (15 ml) oil. Fry, stirring occasionally, until the onions begin to brown, about 5 minutes. Add the hibiscus flowers and maple syrup, turn the heat to low and fry, stirring frequently until the flowers soften, about 5 minutes. Taste the mixture and adjust the maple syrup and salt.

In the meantime, heat the tortillas according to the package directions. Spread some salsa on each one and add a few slices of avocado and a sprinkling of cheese. Spoon the hibiscus mixture overtop, and garnish with sour cream and cilantro. Serve immediately.

TIPS: For a tropical feast, use salsa verde and add lime juice and grilled pineapple as toppings to taste.

You can speed up the process by using a ready-made taco spice mixture.

If you want crispy tortillas, brush the tortillas with oil on both sides. Place them on a baking sheet and bake at 400°F (200°C) until warm, about 4 minutes. Drape the tortillas over a rolling pin and leave to cool.

SERVES 4

2 cups (500 ml) boiling water

2 cups (500 ml) dried hibiscus flowers (see page 176)

3 Tbsp (45 ml) extra virgin olive oil

1 large red onion, thinly sliced

1 clove garlic, finely chopped

1 tsp (5 ml) chili powder

1 tsp (5 ml) ground cumin

1 tsp (5 ml) coarse kosher salt

½ tsp (2 ml) dried oregano

½ tsp (2 ml) paprika

2 Tbsp (30 ml) maple syrup

6 (7-inch/18 cm) flour tortillas

1 cup (250 ml) salsa

1 avocado, sliced

1 cup (250 ml) grated cheddar cheese

Full-fat sour cream (optional)

½ cup (125 ml) chopped cilantro

Dumplings are best made with family or friends on a production line of rolling, folding and love. I lived in South Korea for a couple of years and learned to make dumplings there. My very kind Korean friends were both amused and alarmed by my obsession with dumplings and my ability to eat oh so many of them.

. . . .

Hibiscus Rose Potstickers

To make the filling, place the ingredients in a large bowl and, using a fork or chopsticks, mix together until well combined. Cover and refrigerate until needed.

To make the wrappers, pour ¼ cup (60 ml) of the boiling water into a small heatproof bowl, add the hibiscus flowers and leave to steep for at least 1 hour to make hibiscus tea.

Place 1 cup (250 ml) of the flour in a medium bowl. Pour in the remaining ¼ cup (60 ml) boiling water and ½ tsp (2.5 ml) of the salt. Mix to combine. Let cool enough to handle, knead in the bowl until combined and transfer to a resealable plastic bag to rest at room temperature for 20 minutes. Seal the bag so the dough doesn't dry out.

Strain out the hibiscus flowers from the boiling water, but don't squeeze them or the tea will be bitter. Discard the flowers.

Pour the tea into a medium bowl and mix in 1 cup (250 ml) of the flour and ½ tsp (2.5 ml) of the salt. Wait until the tea is just cool enough to handle and then knead in the bowl until combined. Place the dough in a resealable plastic bag and leave to rest at room temperature for 20 minutes. Seal the bag so the dough doesn't dry out. Take half of the hibiscus dough and half of the plain dough and hand-roll each one into a long, thin log. Place the logs right next to each other on a floured surface and roll them out.

continues

MAKES 8 DUMPLINGS
Photo on page 181

FOR THE FILLING

7 oz (200 g) lean ground pork

2 cloves garlic, finely chopped

¼ cup (60 ml) finely chopped green onions

1 Tbsp (15 ml) minced fresh ginger

FOR THE WRAPPERS

½ cup (125 ml) boiling water, divided

2 Tbsp (30 ml) dried hibiscus flowers (see page 176)

2 cups (500 ml) all-purpose flour, divided

1 tsp (5 ml) table salt, divided

Sesame oil, for frying

Soy sauce, your favorite dipping sauce or wasabi, for serving

The two halves should stick together in the middle so that they make one long piece of dough with the top half pink hibiscus and the bottom half plain dough. Using a 3½-inch (9 cm) circular cookie cutter, cut out 4 round dumpling wrappers. Each wrapper will be half pink and half white. Lay them in a line, slightly overlapping. Lightly wet the wrappers where they overlap with water and press gently so they stick. Place a small scoop of the filling along the center line in a long, thin strip, then moisten the edges of the dough circles and fold the circles in half, from the top to the bottom, pressing gently so they seal. Now roll the filled dough up from left to right to form a rose. Store the dumplings in an airtight container until you are done rolling.

When all the dumplings are formed, place 2 Tbsp (30 ml) of sesame oil in a frying pan and warm it over medium heat. Add all the dumplings to the pan and cook, still over medium heat, for 2 minutes, until the bottoms begin to brown. Pour ½ cup (125 ml) water around the dumplings in the pan and cover. Steam the dumplings for 10 minutes. Remove the lid and drizzle the dumplings with sesame oil, turn down the heat to low and cook for 3 minutes. Remove the pan from the heat. The dumplings are done when a thermometer inserted into the center reads 160°F (71°C). Serve with soy sauce, dipping sauce or wasabi.

HIBISCUS
POMEGRANATE
GIMLET
(page 182)

HIBISCUS ROSE
POTSTICKERS
(page 179)

These perfectly pink ice lollies are a refreshing snack and a great way to get your kids to eat fruit on those hot summer days when you're lying on the grass in the backyard, or when you take a break from swimming in the lake.

. . . .

Hibiscus Watermelon Ice Lolly

MAKES 6 ICE LOLLIES

Place all the ingredients in a blender and blend until smooth.

Pour the mixture into 6 ice lolly molds, leaving a little space for expansion as the liquid freezes. Place in the freezer until frozen and then enjoy!

Store the lollies in the freezer for up to 3 months.

4 cups (1 L) seedless
    watermelon chunks
¼ cup (60 ml) Hibiscus Simple
    Syrup (page 184)
1 tsp (5 ml) freshly squeezed
    lime juice

The gimlet was born in the early 19th century when lime juice rations became compulsory on British ships to combat scurvy. While the crew mixed their daily lime rations with rum, the naval officers mixed theirs with gin to create that G&T we know and love. Thanks to its high vitamin C content, you can enjoy your hibiscus gimlet safe in the knowledge that you are keeping scurvy at bay.

. . . .

Hibiscus Pomegranate Gimlet

SERVES 1

Photo on page 181

Half-fill a cocktail shaker with ice cubes. Add the gin, pomegranate juice, lime juice and simple syrup and shake for 20 seconds. Pour into a coupe glass or martini glass and garnish with a lime twist.

TIP: To make a lime twist, using a vegetable peeler, cut a very thin slice of lime peel. You can do this before juicing so you only use 1 lime for this drink. Using a sharp paring knife, cut the lime peel into a thin strip. Twist the peel into a corkscrew shape.

Ice cubes
3 oz (90 ml) gin
1½ oz (45 ml) pomegranate juice
1 Tbsp (15 ml) freshly squeezed
    lime juice
1 Tbsp (15 ml) Hibiscus Simple
    Syrup (page 184)
Thinly sliced lime twist for
    garnish (optional; see tip)

Granita is a traditional Italian dessert which is a type of sorbet that differs in texture. It's a gem to add to your dessert playbook because it's super easy to make, it's versatile and you can make it from any fruit. Need to level up your margaritas? Just add granita. Your dessert looking a little dull? Granita has your back. Add it to your morning muesli and yogurt, dollop it on top of grilled peaches from the barbecue or just eat it on its own.

. . . .

Hibiscus Strawberry Granita

Place all the ingredients in a blender and blend until the mixture has the consistency of a smoothie.

Place the fruit mixture in a shallow metal baking sheet and set it in the freezer, uncovered, until the mixture just starts to freeze along the top and sides, about 30 minutes. Using a fork, scrape the granita so it looks like flaky snow. Make sure you break up the larger chunks. Return to the freezer and then repeat the scraping process. Freeze and scrape one more time, then freeze for 4 hours before serving.

To serve, leave the granita out on the counter for 20 minutes then use a large serving spoon to scrape it into bowls.

Store the granita in the pan, covered in plastic wrap, in the freezer for up to 1 week.

SERVES 8

Photo on page 188

4 cups (1 L) chopped strawberries

⅓ cup (75 ml) granulated sugar

Pinch kosher salt

1 cup (250 ml) water

3 Tbsp (45 ml) Hibiscus Simple Syrup (page 184)

1 Tbsp (15 ml) freshly squeezed lemon juice

This simple syrup is heavenly. The color alone is enough to seal the deal, but the delicate floral taste is a wonderful addition to your summer drinks, teas and cocktails.

Hibiscus Simple Syrup

Prepare your jars and lids for canning by boiling them in a canning pot for 10 minutes. Using long tongs or a jar lifter, transfer the jars to a wire rack and allow to cool.

Put the boiling water in a large heatproof bowl, add the hibiscus flowers and leave to steep for at least 1 hour to make hibiscus tea.

Strain out the flowers, but don't squeeze them or the syrup will become bitter. Discard the flowers.

Place the hibiscus water in a large pot set over medium heat. Slowly add the sugar, stirring constantly, until it has all dissolved. Bring the cordial to a gentle boil, stirring occasionally for 5 minutes.

Turn off the heat and let the syrup cool. Pour it into the prepared jars. Place the jars in a water bath and boil for 10 minutes. Using canning tongs, carefully remove the jars from the water and allow to cool completely.

Store the syrup in the jars at room temperature for up to 6 months or in the fridge for 1 month after opening.

MAKES 4 CUPS (1 L)
Photo on page 103

4 cups (1 L) boiling water
1 cup (250 ml) dried hibiscus
   flowers (see page 176)
4 cups (1 L) granulated sugar

TIPS: To make a refreshing summer drink, dilute 1 part syrup with 4 parts water or soda water.

In addition to using this syrup for drinks, you can pour this syrup over ice cream, use it as a granita, like on page 183, brush it over your cakes before icing, use it as a pancake syrup or add it to your smoothies. It will make your life at least 3 percent better!

I live in a tiny country town of around 800 people. In my backyard I have a small farm store where I sell jams, jellies, pickles, preserves and other wonderful things made by myself and local residents and farmers. This hibiscus jelly is one of my best sellers, and I'm happy to share the recipe for it here with you. It's a great combination of sweet and sour that makes for a jam that is perfectly balanced.

Hibiscus Jelly

Prepare your jars for canning by boiling them in a canning pot for 10 minutes. Using long tongs or a jar lifter, transfer the jars to a wire rack and allow to cool.

Pour the boiling water into a large heatproof bowl, add the hibiscus flowers and leave to steep for 2 hours to make hibiscus tea. Strain out the flowers, but don't squeeze them, or the jelly will have a bitter aftertaste.

Place the hibiscus tea in a large pot on the stove and stir in the sugar and lemon juice. Bring it to a rolling boil that can't be stirred down.

Stir in the pectin and bring to a boil again, stirring constantly. Boil for 1 minute and then remove from the heat. Leave the jelly to cool in the pot, stirring to ensure all the sugar has dissolved. Skim off and discard any foam from the top of the jelly. Scoop the jelly into the jars and seal lids tightly.

Check the water level in your canning pot, place the jars back in the pot and boil for 10 minutes. Using canning tongs, remove the jars from the water and let cool at room temperature.

Store the jelly at room temperature for up to 1 year, and once opened, in the fridge for 1 month.

MAKES 5–6 CUPS (1.25–1.5 L)

Photo on page 144

4 cups (1 L) boiling water

1 cup (250 ml) dried hibiscus flowers (see page 176)

4 cups (1 L) granulated sugar

1 tsp (5 ml) lemon juice

1 (1¾ oz/49 g) package powdered pectin

TIP: Don't want to use so much sugar? Use diabetic pectin and cut down the sugar to 1–2 cups (250–500 ml) depending on taste. This pectin will ensure the jam sets properly.

Wherever groups of humans have banded together to form societies, they have, at some point, thrown batter into hot oil, fried it up and coated it with something sweet. The very history of humanity is the history of sweet, sweet fried doughs—it's what separates us from the animals. I am honored to perpetuate the proud tradition of the donut, but be warned: once you discover how easy it is to make donuts and how good they are fresh, your life will be forever changed.

. . . .

Hibiscus Jelly Donuts

Place 2 Tbsp (30 ml) of the sugar in a small bowl. Mix in ¼ cup (60 ml) of the water, followed by the yeast. Mix together and set aside until foamy, about 10 minutes.

Transfer the yeast mixture to a stand mixer fitted with the dough hook. In a separate bowl, sift in the flour and salt. Add the dry ingredients and eggs to the yeast mixture and mix on low speed until an elastic dough forms, about 4 minutes.

While the mixer is running, slowly add the butter, one bit at a time, mixing well after each addition, about 6 minutes. Transfer the dough to an oiled bowl and cover with plastic wrap or a damp tea towel. Leave in a warm area and let rise until doubled in size, 45–60 minutes.

Line a baking sheet with parchment paper.

Transfer the dough to a well-floured work surface and punch it down. Roll it out to about ½ inch (1.25 cm) thick. Using a well-floured 2½-inch (6.25 cm) cookie cutter, cut out rounds. You can gather and re-roll the dough until it is all cut into rounds.

Place the donut rounds on the prepared baking sheet and cover. Leave in a warm place until doubled in size, about 45 minutes.

MAKES 10–12 DONUTS

Photo on page 188

½ cup + 2 Tbsp (155 ml) granulated sugar, divided

¼ cup + 1 Tbsp (75 ml) warm water heated to 110°F (45°C), divided

1 envelope (2¼ tsp/11 ml) active dry yeast

1⅔ cups (400 ml) all-purpose flour

1 tsp (5 ml) fine kosher salt

2 large eggs, at room temperature

¼ cup (60 ml) unsalted butter, softened and divided into 6 pieces

Vegetable oil for frying

1 cup (250 ml) Hibiscus Jelly (page 185)

Line a large plate with paper towels.

In a large, deep pot, heat 2 inches (5 cm) of oil (you can use a deep fryer if you have one) over high heat. When the oil reaches 338°F (170°C) on a candy thermometer, using a slotted spoon or a spider, gently place 2 donuts into the oil, making sure not to splash any oil. Only fry a couple at a time, as they cook really quickly and you need to be able to remove them before they burn. Fry until golden brown, just under 1 minute on each side. Using a slotted spoon or spider again, remove the donuts from the oil and place on the prepared plate. The paper towels will absorb any excess oil.

Place the jelly in a piping bag fitted with a #1A tip (see tip on page 42). Gently insert the piping bag tip into the center of a donut and pipe in the jelly until you feel the donut firm up. Remove the piping bag and gently place the donut on your serving platter.

Dust the donuts with the remaining ½ cup (125 ml) sugar and eat one immediately.

Store the donuts in an airtight container at room temperature for 1–2 days.

TIPS: Don't want filled donuts? No problem. Dust with sugar or top with chocolate if you prefer.

You can use a smaller cookie cutter to remove the center of the donuts. This means they will cook more evenly and more quickly—only about 45 seconds per side.

Don't have a candy thermometer? You will know the oil is ready when a small ball of dough placed in the pot of hot oil sizzles and immediately floats to the top.

HIBISCUS
JELLY DONUTS
(page 186)

HIBISCUS
STRAWBERRY
GRANITA
(page 183)

HIBISCUS POACHED
PEARS WITH MERINGUE
(page 189)

Don't you just love a good pear? A good pear can make your whole day. Unfortunately, pears are perfectly ripe for about 2 minutes on a Tuesday when you're not looking. I buy them almost ripe and firm and poach them in booze or hibiscus tea so I know they are going to be just perfect.

Hibiscus Poached Pears with Meringue

Before you begin, wash the bowl and whisk attachment of your stand mixer in warm soapy water and rinse thoroughly. If there is any grease on your equipment, your meringue won't stiffen.

To make the meringue, using a blender or a mortar and pestle, grind the dried hibiscus flowers into a powder, place them in a small bowl and mix in the water to form a paste.

Preheat the oven to 225°F (105°C). Line 2 baking sheets with parchment paper.

Using a stand mixer fitted with the whisk attachment, whip the egg whites, cream of tartar and salt on low speed until foamy, about 4 minutes.

Turn up the mixer speed to high and add the sugar, 1 Tbsp (15 ml) at a time, while it's running. Mix for 15–20 seconds after each addition so the sugar is incorporated before you add the next spoonful. Whip until the mixture is shiny and stiff peaks have formed.

Using a spoon, gently fold in the hibiscus paste. Don't mix it too much if you want a marbled effect. Spoon or pipe 8 meringue shells in a nest shape about 3 inches (7.5 cm) in diameter onto the prepared baking sheets (4 shells per sheet). For accuracy, you can use a pencil to trace a 3-inch (7.5 cm) cookie cutter onto parchment paper. Repeat for 8 circles. Use a #1A tip in a piping bag to pipe meringue into each circle.

continues

SERVES 8

FOR THE MERINGUE

¼ cup (60 ml) dried hibiscus flowers (see page 176)

4 tsp (20 ml) water

4 large egg whites, at room temperature

½ tsp (2 ml) cream of tartar

⅛ tsp (0.5 ml) coarse kosher salt

1 cup (250 ml) granulated sugar

Bake until crispy on the outside and chewy inside, about 2½ hours. Turn off the oven, prop the oven door open with a wooden spoon and leave the shells to cool like this for 10 minutes. Gradually cooling the shells will prevent cracking.

Meanwhile, to make the pears, place the pears, sugar, hibiscus flowers, cinnamon stick, water and lemon juice in a medium pot. Simmer over medium heat until the pears are soft enough to be eaten with a spoon but still firm enough to hold their shape, about 20 minutes.

Using a slotted spoon, gently remove the pears from the poaching liquid and set aside on a plate to cool for 15 minutes. Strain out the hibiscus flowers, but don't squeeze them or the syrup will be bitter, and return the liquid to the stove.

Reduce poaching liquid over low heat to form a syrup that you can pour over your pear dessert for added sweetness, 15–20 minutes. When ready to serve, place the pears gently on the meringues and spoon the syrup overtop just before serving.

If making ahead, meringues can stored in an airtight container at room temperature for up to 2 days.

FOR THE PEARS

4 pears, peeled, cored and halved (Bosc are best!)

1½ cups (375 ml) granulated sugar

½ cup (125 ml) fresh hibiscus flowers (see page 176)

1 cinnamon stick

2 cups (500 ml) water

3 Tbsp (45 ml) freshly squeezed lemon juice (1–2 lemons)

TIPS: A dollop of cream, mascarpone cheese or ice cream won't go astray here.

Using a melon baller will help you to core pears seamlessly.

There have been many great partnerships through history—Lennon and McCartney, Watson and Holmes, Ben and Jerry—but the undisputed champ of duos has always been peanut butter and jelly. If you think they're great together on sandwiches, just wait until you try them in cookies!

Hibiscus PB&J Cookies

Arrange oven racks in top and bottom third of oven. Preheat the oven to 350°F (175°C). Grease two baking sheets.

Sift the flour, baking soda and baking powder into a large bowl.

Using a stand mixer fitted with the paddle attachment, cream the butter with both sugars on medium speed until light in color, about 5 minutes. Add the peanut butter, egg, and vanilla and mix until well combined.

With the mixer running on medium speed, slowly add the dry ingredients to the butter mixture. Mix until soft, but not sticky.

Scoop 1 Tbsp (15 ml) of the dough into your palm and roll it into a ball. The dough should not stick to your hands. If it's too wet, the cookies will spread. Add a little more flour, 1 Tbsp (15 ml) at a time, until it no longer sticks to your hands. Drop the balls of dough onto the prepared baking sheet, about 1 inch (2.5 cm) apart.

Using your thumb, press down in the center of the dough ball to make a small well, but don't press all the way through. Add a spoonful of hibiscus jelly to the center of each cookie.

Bake cookies in top and bottom thirds of oven until the edges begin to brown, about 9 minutes. Swap baking sheets halfway through baking. Place the baking pan on a wire rack and leave the cookies to cool in the pan.

Store the cookies in an airtight container for up to 3 days.

MAKES 40–48 COOKIES
Photo on page 70

1⅔ cups (400 ml) all-purpose flour
¾ tsp (4 ml) baking soda
½ tsp (2 ml) baking powder
½ cup (125 ml) salted butter, softened
½ cup (125 ml) granulated sugar
½ cup (125 ml) lightly packed brown sugar
¾ cup (175 ml) smooth or crunchy peanut butter (see tip)
1 large egg
1½ tsp (7 ml) pure vanilla extract
1 cup (250 ml) Hibiscus Jelly (page 185)

TIPS: I like hibiscus jelly in these, but you can use any jam you like!

For more perfect-looking cookies, use smooth peanut butter. For a more textured bite, use crunchy. You can add ½ cup (125 ml) chopped nuts if you want extra chunks.

15.

15. GENUS: *CROCUS SATIVUS*   PERRENNIAL

. . . .

IDENTIFICATION:

The fall-flowering saffron crocus isn't found in the wild as it is sterile. The bulbs must be dug up and split manually in order for the plant to reproduce. The plant sprouts 5-11 white leaves, called cataphylls, which protect its true leaves. The leaves are thin, straight and dark green and open with the flower.

The flower is made up of beautiful oblong petals that range from a pastel shade of lilac to a deep mauve and has a sweet, gentle fragrance.

GROWING:

Saffron must be grown in well-drained soil in full sun. They can usually tolerate temperatures up to −14°F (−25°C) and short periods of snow, but can weather more severe winters when planted deep underground.

Plant 100 bulbs per 10 square feet (1 square meter) and fertilize once a year. Saffron doesn't need much water, only about ½ inch (1.25 cm) a week from the time of planting to harvest. Once you have harvested the flowers, you won't need to water the bulbs again.

To harvest, cut the saffron flowers and then remove the 3 bright red stigmas in the center by snipping with a small scissors. Each flower only produces three thin threads which is why this spice is so expensive. Lay the threads on a paper towel in a dry place for 3–5 days until dry. Store in an airtight container for up to 1 year.

Saffron

I'm always excited to see my crocus plants pushing up from the muddy earth. That's because these harbingers of spring are one of the first flowers to poke their heads out after winter. The saffron crocus is a beautiful deep purple with crimson stigma, called threads, which are picked, dried and used as saffron spice. Saffron has always been the most expensive spice by weight, and for good reason. The crocus flowers are unpredictable and pop up in the spring and fall whenever they feel like it—and the flowers only last for a single day before withering.

Saffron farmers therefore must pick the flowers and harvest the threads on the day the plants bloom or lose the crop. I live near a saffron farm, and every year, legions of local residents are on call during the fall season to help with the harvest. It's a great community-building exercise as we slop through the mud to pick the blooms and then sit at long trestle tables harvesting the threads.

I love this combo of veggies which make for a delicious and colorful dish. Saffron adds an earthy, nuanced floral flavor to the dressing that really elevates this classic to new heights. You won't have any trouble eating your veggies with this dressing!

· ·

Roasted Veggie Salad with Saffron

Preheat the oven to 425°F (220°C).

Using a mandolin or a very sharp knife, slice the parsnips, carrots, sweet potatoes and beets into round, paper-thin slices. Place on 2 baking sheets greased with olive oil and drizzle olive oil over the top of the veggies. Season with kosher salt.

Bake until you can poke a fork in them with no resistance, about 8 minutes. Place the roasted veggies in a large serving bowl.

Place the dressing ingredients in a bowl and mix thoroughly. Pour over the veggies and serve immediately.

TIP: I love roasting pumpkin seeds or sunflower seeds in a little olive oil and sprinkling on top for a crunchy element (see page 118).

SERVES 6

Photo on page 173

FOR THE VEGETABLES

3 small parsnips, peeled

6 medium carrots, peeled

2 medium sweet potatoes, peeled

2 medium beets, peeled

Extra virgin olive oil

1 tsp (5 ml) coarse kosher salt

FOR THE DRESSING

2 Tbsp (30 ml) apple cider vinegar

2 tsp (10 ml) Dijon mustard

2-inch (5 cm) piece ginger, peeled and finely chopped

¼ tsp (1 ml) saffron threads (see page 192)

2 Tbsp (30 ml) maple syrup

3 Tbsp (45 ml) extra virgin olive oil

1 small shallot, finely chopped

This is one of my favorite recipes in this book. The pillowy softness of the gnocchi, a little sweetness from the butternut and a little bitter saltiness from the brown butter make for a whole lot of flavor. This dish is decadent, silky and so good, you'll want to hug the chef!

. . . .

Butternut Gnocchi with Saffron Brown Butter

Preheat the oven to 375°F (190°C).

To make the gnocchi, halve the squash and, using a spoon, scoop the seeds. Set the seeds aside. Coat the squash in 2 Tbsp (30 ml) of the oil, place it on a baking sheet and bake until you can poke a fork in it without resistance, 40 minutes. Place the baking sheet on a wire rack and let the squash cool enough to handle.

Remove the skin and, using a blender, puree the squash until smooth. Place the puree in a medium pot and cook gently over medium heat until all the excess water is gone, about 5 minutes. Allow the puree to cool completely in the pot.

Preheat the broiler to high.

Rinse the butternut seeds until they are no longer slimy and all the string has been removed. On a baking sheet, coat the seeds in the remaining 1 Tbsp (15 ml) oil and a little salt. Place under the broiler until lightly toasted, about 15 minutes. Shake the baking sheet halfway through the baking to turn the seeds.

Using a stand mixer fitted with the dough hook, mix the puree, salt, Parmesan and egg on medium speed with just enough flour to form a dough that pulls away from the sides of the bowl. I end up using 2 cups (500 ml) usually, but add the flour ½ cup (125 ml) at a time and see how it goes. It's okay to have a slightly sticky dough—the less flour you use, the softer your gnocchi will be.

continues

SERVES 4

FOR THE GNOCCHI

1 large butternut squash

3 Tbsp (45 ml) extra virgin olive oil, divided

½ tsp (2 ml) coarse kosher salt, plus a little extra for the squash seeds

½ cup (125 ml) grated Parmesan cheese, plus extra for sprinkling

1 large egg, lightly beaten

2 cups (500 ml) all-purpose flour, plus extra for rolling

Divide the dough into 6 evenly sized pieces. On a lightly floured surface, roll each piece out into a long gnocchi snake ½ inch (1.5 cm) wide. Cut each strip into ½-inch-long (1.5 cm) pieces. Use a gnocchi board or a fork to gently press down on each piece to form ridges on the top.

To make the sauce, place the butter, garlic, sage, saffron and a pinch of salt in a frying pan set over medium heat. Cook the butter, stirring continuously, until it starts to turn brown, about 5–8 minutes. Keep tasting it until it starts to taste nutty, adding more salt if needed, taking care not to burn it.

Meanwhile, bring a large pot of salted water to a boil over high heat. Gently add the gnocchi in a single batch and cook until they float to the top—it won't take long, just a few minutes. Gnocchi are delicate, so remove them from the water with a slotted spoon rather than pouring them into a sieve or colander.

Pour the brown butter sauce over your gnocchi, sprinkle with Parmesan and the toasted butternut seeds and serve immediately.

FOR THE SAUCE

½ cup (125 ml) unsalted butter

1 clove garlic, finely chopped

¼ cup (60 ml) coarsely
  chopped fresh sage leaves

1 tsp (5 ml) saffron threads
  (see page 192)

Kosher salt, to taste

BUTTERNUT GNOCCHI
WITH SAFFRON BROWN
BUTTER (page 195)

Fried chicken, how do I love thee? Let me count the ways. The tenderness the buttermilk infuses, coupled with the juicy crispiness of the skin, will make this the best fried chicken you'll ever try.

Ode to Crispy Fried Chicken

To make the marinade, mix the buttermilk, saffron, salt, pepper, cayenne pepper and garlic in a large bowl. Add the chicken pieces to the bowl and marinade in the fridge for 2 hours, or ideally overnight.

About 30 minutes before you're ready to cook, remove the chicken from the fridge and let it come to room temperature.

To make the dredge, place the flour, paprika, salt, pepper and cayenne pepper in a large bowl and mix together. Take the chicken, one piece at a time, and dredge in the flour mixture, pressing the chicken lightly into the flour mixture so it sticks nicely. If you have time, let the chicken stand for 30 minutes before frying. This helps the flour coating to stick to the skin.

Fill a heavy-bottomed pot with 1 inch (2.5 cm) of oil (or use a deep fryer, if you have one). Heat the oil to 325°F (160°C) over high heat and fry the chicken in batches until the internal temperature reaches 165°F (74°C), turning once, 15–18 minutes in total.

Enjoy the crispy, sweet and hot flavor with a cold beer and a good friend.

TIP: Peanut oil has a high smoke point which makes it excellent for frying chicken. It has a very subtle flavor that won't interfere with the flavor of your chicken.

SERVES 6

Photo on page 174

FOR THE MARINADE

3 cups (750 ml) full-fat buttermilk

1 tsp (5 ml) saffron threads (see page 192)

2 Tbsp (30 ml) coarse kosher salt

1 Tbsp (15 ml) freshly ground black pepper

½ tsp (2 ml) cayenne pepper

1 clove garlic, finely chopped

4 lb (1.8 kg) medium chicken pieces (wings, thighs and drumsticks)

FOR THE DREDGE

2 cups (500 ml) all-purpose flour

1 tsp (5 ml) smoked paprika

1 tsp (5 ml) coarse kosher salt

1 tsp (5 ml) freshly ground black pepper

½ tsp (2 ml) cayenne pepper

Vegetable or peanut oil, for frying

Saffron beer cheese dip. If this isn't the best phrase ever written, I don't know what is! So many delicious elements combine to make what is truly a divine dip for crisps, crusty bread or veggies. Just eating it with a spoon is also fine.

· ·

Saffron Beer Cheese Dip

Place the cheddar and cream cheese in a skillet and mix in the garlic and beer. Season to taste with the salt, saffron and cayenne pepper. Gently heat the mixture over medium heat until the cheese melts, stirring occasionally. Garnish with chives and serve warm.

SERVES 8

Photo on page 135

3 cups (750 ml) grated
  cheddar cheese
8 oz (225 g) brick-style cream
  cheese, softened
2 cloves garlic, finely chopped
1 cup (250 ml) lager beer
Kosher salt
½ tsp (2 ml) saffron threads
  (see page 192)
¼ tsp (1 ml) cayenne pepper
1 Tbsp (15 ml) chopped fresh
  chives, or green onion

CHERRY HAND PIES
(page 202)

SAFFRON CARROT
CAKE (page 201)

I got the original recipe for this cake from Bernadette, a great local home cook, who makes the most delicious carrot cake in the world (fact). The saffron gives the cake an earthy, floral flavor that really balances out all the other flavors. The pineapple brings moistness and a tartness that adds another dimension to the flavor. It's just the best. Promise!

. . . .

Saffron Carrot Cake

Preheat the oven to 350°F (175°C). Grease a 9 × 13-inch (23 × 33 cm) baking pan.

To make the cake, sift the flour, sugar, baking powder, baking soda, cinnamon and salt into the bowl of your stand mixer, add the saffron and whisk to combine. Add the eggs, ½ cup (125 ml) of the reserved pineapple juice and the oil. Mix on medium speed until combined, about 2 minutes. Add the crushed pineapple, carrots and walnuts. Mix well to combine, about 3 minutes. Scrape down the sides and bottom of the bowl as needed. Once the batter is combined, pour it into the prepared baking pan.

Bake until a skewer inserted into the cake comes out clean, about 50 minutes. Place the pan on a wire rack and let the cake cool completely.

To make the icing, place the cream cheese and icing sugar in a medium bowl and mix to combine using a wooden spoon. Remove the cooled cake from the pan, cover with icing and sprinkle with chopped walnuts.

Store any leftover cake in an airtight container for up to 3 days.

MAKES ONE 9 × 12-INCH (23 × 30 CM) CAKE

FOR THE CAKE

2 cups (500 ml) all-purpose flour

2 cups (500 ml) granulated sugar

2 tsp (10 ml) baking powder

1½ tsp (7 ml) baking soda

1½ tsp (7 ml) ground cinnamon

Pinch table salt

1½ tsp (7 ml) saffron threads (see page 192)

3 large eggs

1 cup (250 ml) drained, crushed pineapple (juice reserved)

¾ cup (175 ml) canola oil

2 cups (500 ml) grated carrots

½ cup (125 ml) chopped walnuts, plus more for decoration

FOR THE ICING

4 oz (125 g) brick-style cream cheese, softened

1 cup (250 ml) icing sugar

Hand pies are the sandwich version of a pie. You can eat a hand pie anywhere—on the run, in the bath or while floating down a river on an inner tube. No need for forks or plates or slices that come apart when you dig into them. Hand pies are portable, baby! So now you really can have your pie and eat it anywhere you please. The tartness of the cherries in this pie balance out the sweetness of the syrup. The earthy floral notes of the saffron take the whole thing to new heights.

Cherry Hand Pies

To make the dough, place the flour, sugar, baking powder and salt in a medium bowl and mix to combine. Using your fingertips, rub in the shortening until it resembles fine breadcrumbs. Add the water, a little bit at a time, until the dough comes together. Do not overwork the dough. Shape the dough into a disk, cover it with plastic wrap and refrigerate for 20 minutes.

To make the filling, place the cherries, water, lemon juice, sugar, saffron and cornstarch in a pot and bring to a boil over medium heat, stirring occasionally. Turn down the heat to low and simmer, stirring frequently for 10 minutes, until the mixture begins to thicken. Remove from the heat and let the filling cool in the pot.

On a lightly floured work surface, roll out the dough to ⅛-inch (0.25 cm) thickness on a clean surface dusted with flour. Use a glass or cookie cutter to cut out 3-inch (7.5 cm) rounds—you should get 16 rounds total. Gather and re-roll the dough as needed. Place 2 Tbsp (30 ml) of the cherry pie filling in the center of a dough circle. Place another circle on top and press the edges together with a fork.

MAKES 8 HAND PIES

Photo on page 200

FOR THE PASTRY

2 cups (500 ml) all-purpose
   flour, plus a little extra
   for dusting

2 Tbsp (30 ml) granulated sugar

1 tsp (5 ml) baking powder

½ tsp (2 ml) coarse kosher salt

⅓ cup (75 ml) vegetable
   shortening

6 Tbsp (90 ml) water, at
   room temperature

Place the oil in a heavy-bottomed pan and warm it over low heat. Working in batches, fry the pies on both sides until golden brown, 2–4 minutes on each side. Remove from the pan and let cool. Dust with the remaining 2 Tbsp (30 ml) sugar.

Store in an airtight container in the fridge for up to 3 days.

FOR THE FILLING

5 cups (1.25 L) fresh pitted cherries

½ cup (125 ml) water

2 Tbsp (30 ml) freshly squeezed lemon juice

⅔ cup (150 ml) granulated sugar

1 tsp (5 ml) saffron threads (see page 192)

¼ cup (60 ml) cornstarch

½ cup (125 ml) vegetable oil, for frying

2 Tbsp (30 ml) granulated sugar, for dusting

TIPS: You can use frozen pastry instead of making your own. Crescent roll pastry works well too. Whipped cream or ice cream would not go astray with these pies.

SAFFRON PEACH PIE
(page 206)

A sweet peach is everything good about summer—like running downhill at full speed in the sunshine, arms outstretched. I love to make this pie seasonally and will wait with bated breath until I find out that plump, fuzzy peaches have finally arrived at the market. The marriage of peaches and saffron is heavenly. The saffron adds depth and rounds out the flavor with savory notes that balance the sweetness of peaches perfectly.

. . . .

Saffron Peach Pie

To make the crust, place the flour and salt in a medium mixing bowl. Using your fingertips, rub in the shortening until the mixture resembles bread crumbs. Gradually add ⅓–⅔ cup (75–150 ml) ice water—just enough until the dough holds together when pressed. Do not overwork the dough. Divide the dough into 2 evenly sized pieces, cover them with plastic wrap and refrigerate for 1 hour.

To make the filling, place the peaches and both sugars in a bowl and set aside to sit, uncovered, at room temperature for 30 minutes.

Preheat the oven to 400°F (200°C). Grease a 9-inch (23 cm) pie dish.

On a lightly floured surface, roll out half the dough to a 12-inch (30 cm) circle, then carefully transfer it to the pie dish.

Gently work it into the edges and up the sides of the dish, and trim off the excess. Prick the bottom of the dough 7–10 times with a fork, then line loosely with parchment paper and fill to the brim with baking beans or pie weights. Bake for 7–10 minutes then remove from the oven. Leave to cool.

Baking the crust for 10 minutes before filling helps to prevent a soggy bottom.

MAKE ONE 9-INCH (23 CM) PIE

Photo on page 204

FOR THE PIE CRUST

2½ cups (625 ml) all-purpose flour

½ tsp (2 ml) coarse kosher salt

1 cup (250 ml) vegetable shortening

⅓–⅔ cup (75–150 ml) ice-cold water

FOR THE FILLING

6 sweet peaches, peeled and sliced

½ cup (125 ml) granulated sugar

¼ cup (60 ml) lightly packed brown sugar

3 Tbsp (45 ml) cornstarch

¼ tsp (1 ml) ground nutmeg

1 tsp (5 ml) saffron threads (see page 192)

¼ tsp (1 ml) ground cinnamon

Pinch table salt

2 tsp (10 ml) freshly squeezed lemon juice

1 Tbsp (15 ml) salted butter

Strain the peaches and place any remaining peach juice, cornstarch, nutmeg, saffron, cinnamon and salt in a medium pot. Bring to a boil, stirring occasionally on medium heat. Reduce heat to low and simmer gently, stirring constantly, until the mixture thickens, about 2 minutes. Add the lemon juice and butter and stir until the butter melts and mixes in with the other ingredients. Add the peaches and gently turn to coat with the cornstarch mixture. Remove from the heat and let cool in the pot.

Spoon the peach mixture into the pie shell. Roll out the remaining dough to a rough rectangle shape about 12 inches (30 cm) long and cut into 1½-inch-wide (about 4 cm) strips. Create a lattice pattern on the top and pinch the edges. Loosely cover the edges with foil and bake the pie for 40 minutes. Remove the foil and bake until the crust is golden brown, about 10 minutes.

Cool completely before serving.

Store leftover pie in a sealed container in the fridge for up to 3 days.

TIP: To peel the peaches, make an X on the bottom with a paring knife. Pop the peach into boiling water for 30 seconds, then peel the skin off.

A kitchen blowtorch is a wonderful thing. There is nothing more delightfully satisfying than watching sugar brown and bubble as you torch the top of a crème brûlée. If you don't have a torch, use your broiler. These delectably smooth, delicious desserts will be none the worse for it. Am I going to say anything about the bacon bits? They need no introduction. . .

Saffron Crème Brûlée with Candied Bacon Bits

Preheat the oven to 325°F (160°C). Grease a baking sheet.

To make the crème brûlée, using a sharp paring knife, split the vanilla bean lengthwise and scrape out the paste. Place the paste and pod in a medium pot, mix in the cream and then the saffron. Bring to a boil (without stirring) over high heat. Remove the pot from the heat and set aside to cool for 15 minutes. Remove the vanilla bean pod (see tip).

Using a stand mixer fitted with the whisk attachment, whip ½ cup (125 ml) of the sugar with the egg yolks on medium speed until light in color, about 3 minutes. Add the cream and saffron mixture a little at a time, whisking continuously until incorporated. Pour the mixture into 6 ramekins, each able to hold ½ cup (125 mL). Carefully place them in a large roasting pan. Fill the roasting pan with enough hot water to reach halfway up the sides of the ramekins, making sure you don't splash any water into the ramekins.

Bake until the crème brûlée is just set but still wobbly in the middle, about 40 minutes. Remove the roasting pan from the oven, but leave the oven on. Place the crème brûlées in the fridge for 2 hours to set.

continues

SERVES 6

FOR THE CRÈME BRÛLÉE

1 vanilla bean

4 cups (1 L) whipping (35%) cream

1 tsp (5 ml) saffron threads (see page 192)

1 cup (125 ml) granulated sugar, divided

6 large egg yolks

FOR THE BACON BITS

3 slices lean bacon

¼ cup (60 ml) granulated sugar

LAVENDER LOVE
MARTINI
(page 101)

SAFFRON CRÈME BRÛLÉE
WITH CANDIED BACON
BITS (page 208)

To make the bacon bits, increase oven temperature to 400°F (200°C). Lay the bacon on the prepared baking sheet and cook in preheated oven until very crispy, about 10–15 minutes. Pat gently with paper towel to remove any grease and leave to cool completely on the baking sheet. Break it into small pieces once it has cooled.

Lay a piece of parchment paper large enough to hold the bacon bits without crowding on your work surface.

Place the sugar in a small pot and melt it over low heat, stirring gently as it melts. Remove the pot from the heat and stir in the bacon bits. Pour the bacon bits out onto the parchment paper and leave to cool.

Remove the crème brûlées from the fridge 30 minutes before you plan to serve them (see tip). Sprinkle the remaining ½ cup (125 ml) sugar evenly overtop of each custard and melt with a blowtorch until golden brown. The darker the brûlée, the more bitter it will be.

If you don't have a blowtorch, you can set the oven to broil, sprinkle the sugar over the custards and set the oven rack so they are about 4–6 inches (10–15 cm) away from the element. Place the ramekins on a baking sheet and broil until golden brown, 5–6 minutes. Keep a close eye on them to avoid burning.

Garnish with bacon bits just before serving.

TIPS: Use vanilla bean pods to flavor sugar. Simply rinse the pod off, leave to dry, then add to your sugar pot to gently flavor your sweet treats.

Once you've baked your crème brûlées, you can leave them to set in the fridge for up to 3 days. This makes it the perfect dessert to make before a big event to reduce your workload on the day.

Acknowledgments

And the "thank you" goes to:

The best publishers in the known world, Lindsay Paterson and Robert McCullough

BFF and MVP Dana Harrison who was the heart of this project (@thatdanaharrison)

My sweet taste-tester Ian Fotheringham

Laura Berman, photographer extraordinaire (@greenfusephotos)

Our food stylist, Ruth Gangbar (@ruthgangbar)

Blacksmith Douglas Morlock for the finest shears and knives (@douglas_morlock_blacksmith)

Marie Alexander for fresh veggies and inspiration

Dr. Kent Tisher for the beautiful roses

Chocolate savant Angela Roest for the most decadent chocolate (@center.and.main.chocolate)

Raquilda van Zoeren for the beautiful dishes (@thevillagepantry)

Monica Johnson for the same (@franticfarms)

Hazel Joan Spot for the beautiful hand-stitched linens

Randy Pearle and Jackson Thurling for the antique dishes (@jacksonandrandy)

Lenni Workman for the amazing flowers (@artfarmproduce)

Terry Grundy for the editing

Jill Proudfoot and Bruce Weir for the honey (@blacktractorfarms)

Index